Building Power in Babylon

COURTNEY SHARPE

DEDICATION

To all the powerless in the world,
and to those boldly striving for power in a society that tries
to limit them.
This is for the ones who refuse to stay down,
who rise despite the odds, and who dare to build power
where they were never meant to.

CONTENTS

ACKNOWLEDGMENTS

I want to begin by expressing my gratitude to Kelvin Osondu from KayVee Books for helping bring this book to life. His hard work, creativity, and unwavering resilience played a key role in shaping this powerful piece of work.

I am truly grateful for his dedication throughout the entire process. He is a part of history in the making, for a better today and an even greater tomorrow

Introduction

———-

In this book, we'll explore how to build power in Babylon, meaning the modern-day society we live in today. When I talk about building power in society, I'm speaking from the perspective of rising from the bottom and reaching the highest levels of status, power, and influence over everyday people.

I'm not talking about being an online influencer with a big following of people who aren't doing anything with their lives. Building power is not for those fooled into thinking that listening to so-called influencers inspires them, only to log off and still feel stuck inside.

Building power is for those who are ready to take it into their own hands by doing the work, no handouts. It's for those bold enough to rise on their terms, without apology. It's for those who want to create real, human-to-human influence, the kind that moves people to action, that gives clear instructions and inspires others to rise and be part of a revolutionary change for the good of all humanity.

Chapter 1

―――

Create Your Voice

To build power in Babylon, you must first create a voice that matters to the people you're trying to build with. Your voice needs to connect with them deeply. It should inspire real change, not just for yourself, but for the betterment of their lives. Your voice can't come from a selfish place. It has to be selfless, a voice for the everyday person looking for a way out of Babylon.

Creating that kind of voice in today's climate isn't easy. Social media has made it possible for anyone to speak, which might sound great in theory, but in reality, it's flooded with noise. There are too many people using their voices for empty, clickbait content, chasing likes, followers, and attention without offering anything meaningful. These are wasted voices. And when those voices go viral, it becomes harder for real, powerful messages to break through.

So, how do you create a revolutionary voice in a world full of noise? Let's look at one way to do it.

Document Your Voice of Knowledge into a Book

These days, many people use YouTube to share knowledge or their philosophy. It's a great platform, especially for podcasters or anyone building a brand. But here's the question: if YouTube shut down tomorrow, what would happen to your platform? What about the followers and subscribers you've worked so hard to build? Where would they go to hear your message? What if you needed to take a break from posting, what happens to your voice then?

That's the risk of relying solely on online platforms. If you stop showing up, your presence fades. Other influencers come in and fill the gap; some might even take your ideas and pass them off as their own. They could win over your audience and rise faster than you did. The online world moves quickly, and if you don't keep up, your influence can vanish just as fast.

This is why it's powerful to document your voice in a book. A book cements your message in a permanent form. It becomes something no one can take from you. If your book connects with readers, if it spreads and sells across the world, then your voice becomes even stronger. You'll reach people on a deeper level, and they'll carry your message forward.

Look at the great philosophers and leaders of the past. Many are long gone, but their voices still speak through the words they wrote. Their books live on, influencing lives and movements years later. That's legacy. That's power.

Even when you're gone, your voice can still speak through your written words, echoing across generations, across nations. That's what it means to build power in Babylon, even in a world designed to keep you at the bottom.

Importance of Documenting Your Voice into a Book

To build power in Babylon, you must understand the importance of documenting your voice in a book. This is about permanently stamping your voice into society through your writing. It also helps to create long-term power and influence around your name. Depending on how strong your influence becomes, this can turn into a legacy that gets passed from one generation to the next. For example, if you are building power within your family, it makes sense to pass that legacy down. This helps to protect and grow power within the family line.

The message here is simple. Documenting your voice in a book lets you cement your thoughts and ideas into the world. Whether your message is a philosophy that will spark change in years to come or something you want to share with the current generation, a book allows your voice to spread across time and space.

Build Credibility

Building power requires credibility that people can trust. You need some kind of proof or transparency to show that you are who you say you are. Power is not built alone. You will need to connect with others to achieve it. And for that to happen, your credibility is going to matter.

One way to show credibility is by proving your ability to produce real results. Some people do this with a website that displays the work they've done over the years. Others show that they can work with people and deliver value. If people can see that you have done real work, they will start to trust you more.

As mentioned earlier, documenting your voice in a book is also a powerful way to show credibility. The words in your book become evidence of your thinking, your message, and your ability to influence others. Your book becomes a physical form of your voice. It proves that you have something to say and that your message matters. The point is this: without credibility, there is no trust. And without trust, there is no power. If the people you are trying to reach do not trust you, then influence and unity will not happen.

Understanding the Struggles That Come with Building Power

On the journey to building power, some struggles come with this kind of mission, and they must be understood. Without understanding these challenges, you could fall before you even begin to rise. Let's take a look at some of the struggles you may face when trying to build power.

#1 - Jealousy

On your rise to power, you may face jealousy along the way. Do not expect everyone to show you love and support as you climb higher. You might be surprised by who the jealousy comes from. Sometimes it will be your own family, maybe even close friends. A lot of the time, it's the people closest to us that can become our downfall. We often believe those around us will support us, but sometimes the opposite happens.

Jealousy works like a disease. When it reaches its highest point, it can cause someone to act out of character if they don't know how to control it. The lesson here is simple. Keep an eye on the people closest to you, because their jealousy can affect you the most. Be ready to deal with it as you move forward on your journey to power.

#2 - Acceptance of Your Leadership

When rising to power, understand that some people around you, and even some outside of your circle, might struggle to accept your leadership. There are many reasons why this can happen. First, when you decide to build power, you are stepping into a leadership role. You are taking control and trying to rise in status.

If you are someone coming from the bottom, people's expectations of you are usually low. They haven't seen you operate at a high level before, so it might be hard for them to now see you as a leader. Some people will accept your leadership right away, while others might come around later when they see how consistent and capable you are. But some may never accept it.

This is especially true in a modern Babylonian society like ours, where true leadership is rare. We have been without real, trustworthy leaders for a long time. That's why things feel so chaotic. And just to be clear, I'm not talking about online influencers with big followings or corrupt politicians who offer false hope. I'm talking about real leaders who work for the good of humanity.

#3 - The Behaviour of Your Current Surroundings

When building power in Babylon, it's important to pay attention to the behaviour of the people around you. As your power and status rise, the way people behave around you will start to change. That change can be positive or negative.

The key is to keep watching your surroundings while you grow. That way, if you spot any behaviour that could harm your mission, you can deal with it quickly before it causes damage.

#4 - Pain and Suffering

Anyone aiming to build power must accept that the journey comes with pain and suffering. If you think it's going to be easy or filled with fun moments, let me tell you now, it won't be. Rising to power demands sacrifice. You may face situations you never thought you would. Much of the pain might come from betrayal by people you trusted to support you. This could be close friends, family members, or even a partner.

To survive this, you need thick skin. The journey to power is not for the weak or overly sensitive. But if you do consider yourself a sensitive person, don't worry. Later in this book, we'll go through simple ways to numb your pain and build understanding so you can stay focused and complete this mission if you are truly serious.

#5 - Transitioning to Power

The transition into power won't be smooth. Expect a bumpy road with unexpected twists and turns. It will shake up your personal life. It may either make you stronger or break you down.

There is no set formula for how this experience will play out. It depends on your lifestyle before stepping into power. It depends on how well you handle pressure, how solid your character is, and how much strength and stamina you have as a person. There are other factors too, but those are key. If you are in the middle of your transition or about to begin, I truly wish you the best of luck.

#6 - Sabotage of Your Rise to Power

One of the last struggles you will face on your rise to power is sabotage from people around you. If you're coming from a disadvantaged background, your first battles will usually be with the people in your immediate environment. As I've mentioned before, it's often those closest to you who cause the most damage.

Sabotage can show up in many different ways, and you need to be alert. The people trying to sabotage you may not always be obvious. Some will do it directly, while others will act in secret. It's important to recognise the different forms this can take so you can protect yourself early on.

Let's look at a few ways people around you might try to sabotage your rise to power.

(a) Doubt Your Abilities

When it comes to your ability to build power in Babylon, you need to be sure of yourself. This doesn't mean you should be arrogant, although some people might see it that way. That could be due to their own ignorance or because they're not used to dealing with someone who carries high self-esteem.

Unfortunately, many people will doubt your ability to rise and build real power in a system that is designed to keep you at the bottom. This kind of doubt is part of the sabotage you'll face on your journey. The best way to fight it is to be confident in your ability to produce results. Confidence and self-assurance will help you beat the odds and overcome the doubt others will throw at you.

(b) Lack of Support

At the start of your rise to power, don't expect overwhelming support. This is very normal, especially when you're coming from the bottom and aiming for the top. That's not to say you won't get any support, but the amount you receive may be minimal in the beginning.

As you rise higher, things will shift. That's when the jealousy from people around you may start to show. In other words, be prepared to carry the weight of your journey alone for a while. Eventually, new supporters will show up, people who truly want to join forces and build with you.

(c) An Attempt to Hold You Back

Another form of sabotage you'll face is when people try to hold you back while you're pushing forward. The more you strive for greatness, the more intense this resistance can become. And just like before, the people doing this will usually be the ones closest to you.

Outsiders don't know enough about you to try and hold you back. It's the ones within your inner circle you need to watch. Always keep an eye on your surroundings, especially as you move up. That's where the danger lies.

(d) Guilt You Into Not Moving Forward

Some people will try to guilt you into slowing down or stopping altogether. They'll say things like, "You won't have time for me anymore," or "You think you're better than me now?" This is emotional manipulation, and it's designed to keep you from growing.

The best way to deal with this is to stay committed to your journey. You must detach yourself from guilt and remain focused on your mission. Let people say what they want, your purpose is bigger than their emotional games.

(e) Not Embracing Anything You Do

Part of the sabotage may come from people who simply refuse to embrace anything you're doing. This can hurt if you're not built with inner strength. Their lack of support might affect your confidence if you're not prepared.

Just remember, this is part of the process. It's disappointing, especially when the lack of support comes from people you thought would be in your corner. But the truth is, many people are stuck in their own jealousy. They're not able to celebrate your growth because they're still battling their own insecurities.

Don't let that stop you. If your rise to power has real purpose behind it, then keep going, no matter who claps or stays silent.

Chapter 2

Build Universal Philosophy

To build power, you need to understand that this is not something you can do alone. You will need to work side by side with people to rise. To make that happen, you need to create a revolutionary philosophy that is universal, something that speaks to everyone. If you limit your philosophy to one group in society, your impact won't be as strong as it could be. We live in a divided world, split into different factions, so it would be wise not to build your message for only one type of person.

Here are a few key principles that should be part of your revolutionary philosophy:

#1 - Unity

Unity is a powerful principle that can bring people together if it's used with the right knowledge, mindset, and wisdom. When building power, you must have the intention to unite with others who are willing to be part of your journey. You need to carry a unifying mindset, one that sees people as allies and not just supporters. Without unity, your rise to power will fail. Keep this in mind at all times.

#2 - Understanding

Understanding is a key part of building power. You must take the time to understand the people who are walking this journey with you. That means learning how they think, knowing their personalities, and seeing how your vision of power affects their lives, their families, and society as a whole.

You also need to understand what this mission means for you. What impact will building power have on your own life? What is the true purpose of your rise? Without this deeper understanding, it's easy to get lost in the battles, challenges, and changes that come with this journey. Building power will change your life, for better or for worse, so make sure you know exactly what you're walking into.

#3 - Purpose

When building power in Babylon, you must stay focused on your purpose. This is not a game, and it should not be used to hurt or destroy others. The goal is not to act like a tyrant or a dictator. The purpose of building power is to bring real change, for yourself and for others, that will have long-term benefits.

To do that, you need to have the right mindset about what you're going to do once you achieve power. Power without purpose will corrupt you. It will cause you to self-destruct, and that defeats the whole reason why you started this journey in the first place.

#4 - Emotional Discernment

On your rise to power, emotional discernment is crucial. You must be able to manage your emotions and keep a balanced state of mind. If you can't do this, your emotions will control you, and that will ruin your chances of success. Building power is not for people who are emotionally unstable. Power is for those who are grounded and can make hard decisions based on logic, not feelings.

To build power, you must be emotionally fit. If you're dealing with emotional wounds or instability, it may not be your time yet. Go back to the basics. Start your personal development journey and begin your healing process. If you're unsure how to begin, go back to my first book, **How to Survive in Babylon,** and read Chapter 6, Section 6 on healing. Study it and apply the principles. Use that as a guide to deal with the emotional wounds that may be holding you back. Once you've healed, you'll be better equipped to lead with emotional strength and clarity.

Military State of Mind

To build power in today's modern society, you need to have a military state of mind. Think of yourself as an army general leading a group of soldiers. To maintain this mindset, you must stay focused, organised, consistent, and disciplined.

At this point in your life, your approach needs to be from a military standpoint. You'll need to engage in something close to military science. That's because as you build power, enemies will come at you from all directions, and their moves won't always be predictable. You'll need to use strategy, structure, and discipline to stop them from breaking your focus and destroying your progress.

You must keep a military state of mind all year round. Some people may think this is impossible in a society that encourages comfort, weakness, and a docile mindset. But that's exactly why this mindset is important. It gives you mental ammunition to protect yourself from the constant attacks, especially the quiet ones that come from the system itself.

This is not a short-term journey. Building power takes years, and you'll need strength and discipline to stay the course. A military state of mind helps you stay strong by generating a powerful energy force inside your mind and body. It creates a certain presence. People will sense that you're on a mission, that you're serious, and not someone to play with.

Think about a time in your life when you had a clear task and were determined to finish it. Someone might've looked at you and said, "You look like someone on a mission." They could see it in your eyes, your face, and your body language. That's the kind of focus and seriousness you need to carry every day.

This mindset is not a one-time thing. It's a discipline you must renew year after year. If you're serious about building power, then your mind must stay sharp and focused, always.

Offer an Incentive to the People

When building power, especially with everyday people, one of the smartest things you can do is offer an incentive. If you want people to work with you and stay motivated, you need to give them a reason to believe in what they're doing.

Incentives can inspire people to stay committed and perform well. They make people feel seen and valued for the work they put in. When people feel appreciated, they are more likely to give their best. You don't want to cheat or overlook the people helping you. That kind of behaviour breaks trust and weakens your foundation.

This is what the people in power often get wrong. They take from others without giving anything back. You see it in jobs where workers are given more responsibility and longer hours, but no pay rise or reward. That kills morale.

So offering incentives is key. It shows respect and makes people want to keep going with you. But at the same time, be careful not to overdo it. Giving too many rewards too often can spoil people. They may begin to expect it all the time. Some might even try to use that as leverage, demanding more in return for their support, or threatening to walk away if they don't get what they want.

The key lesson is this: incentives are powerful tools to bring the best out of people, but use them wisely and with strategy. Give just enough to keep people motivated, but not so much that they forget the purpose of the mission.

Your Decision Must Be for the Benefit of Your Rise to Power

When you're building power, your decisions must serve the purpose of helping you rise. Understand that not everyone around you will agree with the choices you make and that's okay. It's not your job to manage other people's feelings about your decisions. That would be impossible to do anyway.

During this process, you may fall out with people. Some of the people you were once close to could even become your enemies, all because they don't agree with how you move. Be ready for that. It's part of the journey.

The key is to make decisions from a place of logic and sound reasoning, not emotion. You are not making decisions to keep people happy. You are doing what is necessary to rise to power. And with that rise comes the responsibility to lead and be seen as a person of influence, authority, and respect.

Leave a Legacy

Leaving a legacy before you leave this earth is one of the wisest things you can do. You don't want to be forgotten, because that would make your time here feel like it was all in vain.

Your legacy is not just about you. It's also for your children and your family. And if your impact is strong enough, others who respect you might also carry your legacy forward long after you're gone.

A powerful legacy, if done right, can strengthen your name and your family's name for generations. This is something you should be working on now while you're still alive and building power.

And if you have children, it's your duty to teach them about the legacy you plan to leave behind. Help them understand what it means, why it matters, and how to carry it with the respect it deserves. That way, they can protect it, honour it, and pass it on.

Move in Silence

During your rise to power, it's best to move in complete silence. We live in a time when many people crave attention. Social media is filled with people who want to be seen and heard, chasing clout, likes, and short-term fame. But that type of attention doesn't last, and it has nothing to do with real power.

Building power isn't about going viral or showing off for the cameras. It's about serious, lasting change for yourself, your family, and your community. It's not for playing games online. It comes with real-life consequences. And because of that, you don't want to attract unnecessary attention.

The less people know about what you're doing, the harder it is for them to attack you. Moving quietly protects you. It keeps your plans safe. It gives you time to prepare, to lay strong foundations, and to focus without distractions.

One thing to remember is this: as your power and influence grow, staying silent will get harder. Your name will spread, and people will start paying attention. That's when you'll need to adjust and develop new strategies to protect your moves. But always keep this in mind: moving in silence is not about hiding. It's about staying focused, avoiding distractions, and keeping your power away from unnecessary threats.

Revolutionise How You Start Your New Year

Building power from the bottom of Babylon's society can take years, mainly because of how this system is designed. As many of us already know, Babylon is set up to keep you in a subservient position. That means you can't afford to move like the average person. You have to move differently with more intention, more strategy, and more purpose. If you're serious about building power, you must approach each year in a revolutionary way.

That means you need to give your year a different kind of start what I call a revolutionary start to the new year. This is not just a one-time switch. It's a permanent change in how you kick off every year of your life.

Let's be honest. Most people welcome the new year by counting down 3, 2, 1… "Happy New Year" with alcohol in their hands. Some are already drunk before the clock even strikes midnight. So what happens next? They wake up late on New Year's Day with a hangover and a foggy mind. No goals. No plans. No real vision for how to move forward. And then they wonder why every year feels the same, with little to no progress.

The truth is, when you start your new year with a hangover, you're off to a slow start. You spend most of the day recovering, and by the time your head clears, it's already time to go back to work. Just like that, you're back on the hamster wheel waking up, going to work, and having no time or energy to think about how to move forward. This is where most people get stuck. And it becomes a cycle that repeats itself every single year.

That's why, if you're committed to building power, you need to revolutionise how you begin each year. It could be the shift that changes everything for you. Let's look at a few practical steps to make that happen:

#1 - Start Making Plans for the New Year Two Months Before the Year Ends

One of the fastest ways to gain momentum in the new year is to start preparing at least two months before the current year ends. That gives you time to map out your next move and begin laying the groundwork. Planning gives you a clear path. It brings your vision to life quicker and helps you move with more confidence and direction. This kind of preparation can fast-track your journey to power and set you apart from the crowd.

#2 - Start to Execute Your Plans Before the New Year Starts

Most people wait until January 1st to start working on their goals. That might make sense for the average person, but when you're building power, you don't have time to wait. Power is not built through average thinking.

You need revolutionary thoughts backed by revolutionary action. One powerful move is to start executing your plans before the new year even begins. By doing this, your mindset is already operating in the new year, even though the calendar hasn't flipped yet. That kind of mental shift puts you ahead of the game before it even starts.

#3 - Wake Up on New Year's Day Sober and Ready to Execute

Lastly, wake up on New Year's Day sober and focused. Start the year clear-headed and ready to continue your mission. While others may wake up with hangovers and regret from the night before, you'll be ahead of them, mentally and physically.

If you're serious about building power, avoid entering the new year in a state of confusion. Waking up clear, steady, and prepared gives you a massive advantage. It sets the tone for the rest of your year and the rest of your rise.

Touch the Hearts and Minds of the People

As you grow your influence among everyday people, one important thing you must do on your journey to building power is to touch their hearts and minds. This is a key part of the process because when you touch both the heart and the mind, you create a real connection. That connection builds trust, and once people trust you, your influence and power will grow.

Having the hearts and minds of the people gives you strength. It makes you more confident in your role. There's nothing more powerful than knowing people trust you to lead and believe that your rise in power also empowers them to change their own lives.

Make Yourself a Person People Want to Join Forces With

Building power is never easy, especially when you're starting from the bottom with no name, status, or influence. If you want to build power among the people, it's wise to become someone they want to stand with. You need to be the type of person people are willing to follow and work with.

Ask yourself the following questions:

- Why should people join forces with you?
- What do you have to offer them?
- What can they gain that benefits both you and them?
- What is your purpose in asking people to build with you?

Take time to answer these questions with real thought and context. Doing this will help you understand how to position yourself as someone people want to support.

One more thing, avoid any kind of controlling or forceful

approach. Acting like a dictator only creates division and pushes people away. Power built on fear or control doesn't last. If you truly want to be a force to be reckoned with, work with the people, not against them. That's one of the core principles of building real, lasting power.

Chapter 3

Guard Your Image

When building power in modern-day Babylon, it's highly advisable to be mindful of what you post online, especially on social media. These days, many people are impulsive with how they use social platforms. They post without thinking about how they're presenting themselves to the world. What most people don't consider is the long-term effect of their online content. They forget that one day, they might go through a transformation and evolve into a completely different person.

But by then, it may be too late. Once you post something online, it stays there. It spreads. It circles around and stays accessible for anyone to find.

So, if you're serious about building power among the people, be careful about what you share. Don't post anything that could incriminate you or damage your image down the line. Building power requires strategy, not impulse. In today's world, one wrong post can be used against you, especially if you're up against enemies who want to tear down your influence.

Your online image must stay clean. Treat it like a shield. Because as you grow in power, opposition will come. Do not fall for the illusion that rising to power is an easy ride where you can post anything without consequences. It's not. Be wise with your presence, online and offline.

Don't Look Down on the People You Intend to Build With

When you're building power, never look down on the people you want to build with. This kind of behaviour works against you. If you treat the everyday person like they are beneath you, you risk pushing them away. Some may even turn against you and try to tear down everything you're working on.

Your role is to empower the people, not belittle them. What matters most is whether they're willing to work with you to accomplish the vision. That's what you need to focus on.

People from different backgrounds and lifestyles may want to be part of the power-building process. Your job is to recognise what strengths they bring and how they can contribute to the mission. Power is not built in isolation; it's built through alignment, trust, and shared purpose.

Your Image While Rising to Power Is Important

As you rise to power, your image matters. The way you carry yourself in public, especially among the people you're trying to build with, must command respect and honour. If people don't respect your image or what you stand for, it will be hard to get them on your side.

Carry yourself in a way that people can take seriously. Let your image reflect who you are and what your mission is. But don't confuse this with trying to create a false image just to please others. That won't work.

Your image should be rooted in truth. It's about being authentic and clear about your intentions. Show people the real version of you and how you intend to rise. That's what earns trust.

And to be clear, this has nothing to do with material things or vanity. It's not about clothes, status, or showing off. It's about character. It's about how you think, how you lead, and how you show up for your mission every day. That's the image that matters.

Chapter 4

Recruit the Right People

When building power in Babylon, we must understand that it's not something you can do alone. You have to accept that you'll need to work with other people to help build the power you want to establish.

Working with people means going through a recruitment phase. This phase is all about carefully choosing who you want to work with. Not everyone has the same drive or mindset as you. Some people are comfortable living a mediocre life, even if they're miserable. Many have become conditioned to the modern-day slavery of life, and for them, that has become the norm.

You need to keep this in mind during recruitment. When building power, it's in your best interest to make sure you're partnering with the right people to get the job done. Let's break down how the recruitment phase should work:

#1 - Find Out What the Person Stands For

In the recruitment process, it's important to understand what each person stands for. The goal is to build power with people who have substance. If someone doesn't stand for anything, they'll likely be a problem later on.

You want people with values, vision, and purpose. People who know what they believe in. When you're building a power structure, you need people with character, not just people who are available. Choose those who will strengthen the foundation, not weaken it.

#2 - How Serious Are They About Building Power With You?

You must pay attention to how serious people are about building power with you. This isn't a hobby. This isn't for fun. Building power with purpose is real work.

The best way to figure out if someone is serious is by watching their actions. Look at how they move when they're working beside you. Don't rely on assumptions or words, look at their behaviour. Test them. See how they perform under pressure.

If someone isn't performing to the standard you need, have a conversation with them. See if the issue can be fixed. But if it continues, that may be a sign that they're not taking the mission seriously. And at that point, you may need to replace them with someone more committed.

Don't take it personally. Not everyone is cut out for this kind of work. Not everyone is ready to build power in Babylon. And that's okay. Your job is to find the ones who are.

#3 - Acknowledge Their Strengths and Weaknesses

During the recruitment phase, it's important to recognise the strengths and weaknesses of the people you're going to work with. Doing this helps you truly understand who you're building with. When you know someone's strengths, you can position them in a way that brings the best out of them. And when you acknowledge their weaknesses, you can work with them to improve, or at least make sure those weaknesses don't stop them from performing their role.

Understanding both strengths and weaknesses gives you better control over how your team operates and helps you make smarter decisions about how to use each person effectively.

#4 - Look at What Type of Lifestyle They Live

It's also highly advisable to pay close attention to the lifestyle of the people you're planning to build power with. Whether we like it or not, a person's lifestyle will always have some kind of impact on how they live, work, and perform.

When recruiting people to build power, you need to make sure their lifestyle won't end up becoming a risk or a roadblock in the journey. The reality is, in today's society, many of the people who'll want to work with you won't be coming from perfect lives. You'll be working with everyday people, some struggling, some healing, some still trying to get it together.

Some may come with past trauma. Others might be recovering from addiction. They may be doing better now but are still in fragile stages where relapse or breakdown is possible. That doesn't mean they don't have value, but you need to weigh how their current lifestyle could affect the mission.

The lesson here is to observe closely. If you come across someone whose lifestyle might slow down or disrupt the power-building process, gently let them know it would be best for them to sort those issues out first. Make it clear the door remains open, they can come back when they're in a better place to contribute effectively.

#5 - What Can They Offer?

Always find out what people have to offer. During the recruitment phase, you should be asking each person what skills and strengths they bring to the table. You're not just building a team for the sake of numbers. You need people who bring real value.

Knowing what someone can offer helps you decide what position they should be placed in. Every team needs structure. If someone is strong in one area, put them there. If they have leadership potential, train them for it. The goal is to make sure everyone you recruit plays a meaningful role in helping you rise to the next level of power.

Chapter 5

Participants Not Followers

We live in the age of social media, where people focus heavily on how many followers they have on platforms like YouTube, X (formerly known as Twitter), and Instagram. Having followers online might seem exciting or trendy, but if you really look at what most of those followers are doing, it's just that... They're following. Nothing more.

Many of them spend hours each day watching content from their favourite creators, whether it's on YouTube or other platforms. But when it comes to building real power, followers aren't enough. You need active participants.

You need people who will walk with you, work with you, and be part of the process. Active participants are willing to get their hands dirty and help you build something that lasts. Followers, on the other hand, usually sit back and watch. They often avoid doing the work because it would require them to make real changes in their own lives. And let's be honest, most people in today's society are not ready for that. They've become too comfortable in the privileges and distractions that keep them passive.

Having an Aim

When building power, it's important to have a clear aim. Ask yourself: What kind of power am I trying to build? What is the end goal I'm working toward?

Having an aim gives you direction. It helps you structure your actions in a focused, productive way. It also makes it easier to guide the people who are building with you. When everyone understands the aim, you all move in alignment, and that's how power is built effectively.

Building a Legacy

One of the key ingredients in building power is making sure you leave a strong legacy behind. You want to create something of value that future generations can use to keep moving forward.

Building a legacy is about more than just yourself, it's about securing your place in history. It's about making an impact that lasts, even after you're gone. A strong legacy strengthens your status and influence on earth. It builds respect, not just for who you are, but for what you stood for during your lifetime.

Building Resources

To be successful in building power in Babylon, it's vital that you have the necessary resources. Without resources, your mission becomes ten times harder to carry out. I understand that in today's world, it is becoming more and more difficult to access the tools and support needed to build real power.

But just because it's hard doesn't mean it's impossible.

There are still ways to get what you need. You just have to be intentional and strategic about it. Let's take a look at some of the ways you can go about building and accessing the right resources to support your rise to power.

#1 - Monitor Your Spending Habits

Monitoring your spending habits is something you must do when trying to acquire resources. If you don't keep track of how you spend, you'll struggle to gain anything meaningful. Make sure your spending supports the goal of bringing in resources, not repelling them.

Watching your spending helps you see where your money is going and how it's being used. It also helps you catch any bad financial habits that could hold you back. When you become more aware of your spending, you give yourself the power to change it.

#2 - Don't Waste Money on Things You Don't Need

When trying to build resources, you must avoid wasting money on things you don't actually need. We live in a society that lacks real financial education, and many people throw their money at things that have no lasting value.

You can't build or gather resources if you're constantly spending on things that take away from your financial strength. Every pound spent should serve a purpose.

#3 - Be Resourceful With Your Money

If you're building power in modern-day Babylon, being resourceful with your money is a must. Using your money wisely helps you get closer to your goals. Being resourceful means using your initiative. It means thinking smart, planning well, and stretching every bit of your finances to work in your favour.

This mindset shift is crucial. Too many people in today's world see money as "just paper" because of the way they've been taught to think. But money, when used the right way, becomes a tool, an asset. And in your journey to power, it needs to be treated as one.

#4 - Create a Financial Plan for Attaining Resources

As you build power, it's important to create a financial plan for how you'll gain the resources you need. A clear plan gives you direction. It shows you where your money should go, and it helps you focus on the areas that will actually move you forward.

When you plan properly, you can allocate your money to the right places, places that support growth, progress, and power. Without a financial plan, you might find yourself spending on liabilities instead of assets. And that can delay or even destroy your momentum.

Chapter 6

___

Prepare For Responsibility

Building power is not a light-hearted experience, so I say this clearly, be prepared for the responsibility that comes with it. Most people in today's society have never truly held any form of power in their hands. That's because many have lived their entire lives in subservient positions. They've been conditioned to follow, not lead.

Think about what it means to live in that kind of mindset for your whole life. When someone like that finally starts imagining what it would feel like to have power, they often see it as a fantasy. But the reality is very different from the idea they have in their heads.

Whatever picture you've created in your mind about what building power looks like, expect the real thing to be very different. So if you're not ready to take on that level of responsibility, it might be time to pause and ask yourself if this is really for you. Be honest. This path is not for everyone.

Be Open to Develop New Leadership Skills

Building power means stepping into leadership, whether you realise it or not. The moment you decide to rise, you take on a leadership role. And that means you'll need to constantly grow.

We live in a society that's always evolving. If you don't keep up, you'll get left behind. Developing new leadership skills helps you stay connected to the people you're building power with. It helps you stay relevant and effective.

If you refuse to grow as a leader, you risk falling into outdated ways of doing things. That can cause people to lose faith in your vision. Keep your eyes and ears open. Be ready to shift, adjust, and upgrade your leadership style. That's how you stay in the game and that's how you build lasting power.

Develop a Warrior Mindset

Building power takes strength. It takes resilience. To make it through, you need to develop a warrior mindset. Nothing less will do.

A warrior mindset keeps you grounded through every challenge, every setback, every tough season. You need that mental armour to survive what's coming your way on this revolutionary path.

Without it, you'll break. But with it, you'll rise.

Eradicate the Victim Mindset

When building power in a society that's designed to keep you at the bottom, one of the first things you must do is eradicate the victim mindset. Too many people out here are stuck thinking and acting like victims. That's because they feel powerless in a system that keeps throwing barriers in their way.

You hear it all the time, people saying, "Poor me" or "Why me?" But when you think like a victim, you start acting like one. And when you act like a victim, you convince yourself that you're powerless. That kind of thinking only keeps you weak. And that weak mindset will never help you build power.

If you're serious about this journey, you need to flip the script and develop a stronger mindset. Start by saying these five things to yourself every day:

- I am strong
- I will rise
- I will succeed by any means necessary
- I am unstoppable
- I am a force to be reckoned with

These are not the words of a victim. These are the words of someone ready to take back control. When things get hard, and they will, go back to these five declarations. Let them remind you of who you are and what you're capable of. In a world full of obstacles, you'll need that kind of strength just to stay standing.

Don't Rely on the Government to Help You Build Power

When building power in modern-day Babylon, don't expect the government to help you get there. The truth is, they don't want you to have real power, especially not more than them. So ask yourself this: if they don't want you to rise, why would they ever help you do it? The government wants to keep all the power for themselves. That's the reality.

So if you're serious about building power, you've got to be willing to do it on your own. That means relying on your intelligence, your determination, your resources, and your ability to work with others who believe in the mission.

Don't wait for a handout. Don't expect a boost. Power is something you must build with your own two hands.

Be an Asset to the People

In modern-day Babylon, you must understand that to build power with the everyday person, you first need to be an asset. Being an asset means you're useful, not just to yourself, but to the people you're working with. It makes you valuable. It puts you in demand.

You can't build power if you're a liability. Being a liability means you bring no value, not to others, and not even to yourself. Before you start this journey of building power, ask yourself: why would anyone want to join forces with you if you're not bringing anything useful to the table?

Being an asset could mean having knowledge that helps others grow. It could mean having a skillset that can be shared. Whatever it is, the key is to be someone that others can build with someone who contributes to the mission.

Create a Working Ethos for the People to Work With

When building power among everyday people, it's important to create a working ethos. That means you need a clear set of values, principles, and guidelines that everyone can follow. These should align with your vision and the kind of power you're trying to build.

Your ethos should come from a revolutionary mindset, it should be about creating real change. And just as important, it should be universal. A universal ethos brings people together, makes sure no one feels excluded, and gives everyone a common ground to work from.

When people are united under one clear ethos, things move forward with strength and purpose.

Be Emotionally Intelligent When Exchanging Ideas

As you build power with others, you'll find yourself exchanging a lot of ideas. During this process, disagreements will happen, and that's normal. Not everyone will see things the same way, and that's okay.

What's important is how you handle those disagreements. Don't get caught up in your emotions. You're not here to fall out with people over ideas. An idea is just that an idea. It's not set in stone. It's not the final plan.

So when different opinions come up, stay grounded. Listen. Be open. Focus on the bigger picture. Emotional intelligence during these moments will keep the group strong and focused on the goal building power together.

Revolutionary Thinking Is Needed When Building Power

If you're serious about building power in today's world, you need revolutionary thinking. This is not the time for average or comfortable ideas. Power requires bold, unorthodox thinking, the kind that challenges the norm and breaks through barriers.

To build power, you must train your mind. Educate yourself with the highest levels of revolutionary thought you can find. Mediocre thinking won't help anyone rise. It will keep you stuck at the bottom, far from your full potential.

The message here is clear: if your thinking is still stuck in the old ways, it's time to upgrade. Start reading. Start studying. Start learning revolutionary theory and use it to elevate your mind, and your mission.

Don't Operate Like the Average Person

Building power is a serious task. You need to understand that you cannot operate like the average person if you're going to take this path seriously.

The average person usually just goes to work, comes home, eats dinner, chills out for the evening, then goes to bed only to wake up and repeat the same thing the next day. This becomes a cycle, week in and week out, year after year. And by the time you realise how repetitive it's been, years have passed, and not much has changed. That's the reality for most people.

If you want to build power, you have to go in the opposite direction.

The society we live in encourages you to be like everyone else to play it safe and stay in line. But the philosophy of building power is different. It calls you to operate on a higher level not to look down on others, but to activate the power within yourself and use it fully, no matter what obstacles are placed in your way.

Use Your 9–5 Job to Build Up Resources

In today's world, where money is tight for the average person, you've got to find ways to get the resources you need to build power. Most people don't have a business or a side hustle. Their 9–5 job is all they've got.

You might have seen videos online saying 9–5 jobs are a trap, that they offer no legacy, and that your job can't be passed down to your children. And while that's true, if you don't have a business or extra income yet, your job is still a tool one you can use to fund your rise to power.

Start by looking at your monthly spending. Where can you cut back? What expenses can you reduce? Once you figure that out, take the leftover money and put it towards the resources you need to move forward.

The lesson here is simple: if you're smart with your money, your job can work for you. All it takes is some basic financial literacy and discipline. Use what you have now to get what you need to build power later.

Operate Outside of Societal Parameters

To build power, you'll need to operate outside of society's usual boundaries. What that means is you must step away from the routines and patterns that have been laid out for the everyday person.

Take this example: most people go to work, come home, relax, go to bed, and do it all over again the next day. It's a cycle that repeats week after week. Now look at how the government operates, their system runs 24 hours a day, even while most people are sleeping. When they make plans, they're thinking 50 to 100 years into the future. That kind of long-term planning is far from the mindset of the average person who is stuck in survival mode, only focused on getting through today.

If you're serious about building power, you have to start thinking and operating differently. Instead of going out every weekend to party, spend that time planning your next move. Read books that challenge and empower your mind. Build a personal philosophy that aligns with your mission. Reflect on how to change your current situation for the better.

Here are a few practical ways you can start operating outside of societal parameters:

- Think completely opposite to how most people in society think
- Stand on your own principles, ones that work for you
- Take on new challenges that stretch and grow you
- Stay focused and fix your mind on the mission of building power
- Never compromise who you are during the process

Stepping outside of society's script is the beginning of building something greater.

Chapter 7

———

Mission Over Everything

On your crusade to build power, it's important that you build your own power from within. I say this because most people in modern-day society don't fully understand what it means to build power for themselves.

First, you need to understand that if someone else gives you power, that same person can also take it away. And when that happens, it can leave you feeling inadequate and powerless. When someone knows you're powerless without them, they're more likely to take advantage of you.

That's why it's so important to arm yourself with your own power.

Building your own power from within is a lifelong process, it doesn't stop. It's a continuous journey of growth, self-awareness, and strength. Power is not something you wait to be handed. It's something you create and maintain yourself.

Building power includes a few key things we're going to look at below:

- Knowledge of self
- Knowing your ability to execute tasks
- Learning from others
- Emotional intelligence

- Prioritising your mission as top priority

Become One of the Most Dangerous People

When building power, you should aim to become one of the most dangerous people to walk the earth. Some people might stop and ask, "Why would I want to be dangerous?" Let's break this down for those questioning the idea.

Ask yourself this, is the government not dangerous? If you break the law, don't you face consequences? If you interrupt the current power structure and the control they hold over society, you'll quickly see just how dangerous they can be.

Start studying how much control they actually have in the workplace, the police force, the banks, the school system, the media, the pharmaceutical companies, and even the drug trade. Yes, believe it or not, they have influence there too. What makes the power structure dangerous is that they have their hands in so many sectors of society. And when you look beyond the surface, you'll see that they control a large part of our lives simply because we rely so much on the services they provide.

That's why the average person stuck at the bottom needs to start thinking about gaining some leverage in this structure. If you don't build power for yourself, you'll keep being dominated, and that's exactly what's happening to many people across the world today.

Now let me be clear. I'm not saying you should go out and become a tyrant or do harm to others. I'm saying be dangerous in a way that makes people think twice before trying to take advantage of you. Be the kind of person whose presence commands respect, especially if you're in a position of power.

Being dangerous also means you're not easily manipulated, you're not brainwashed, and you don't live in victim mode. You don't walk around feeling sorry for yourself. You are self-aware and grounded in the strength you carry.

Let's now look at a few things that can help you become one of the most dangerous people.

#1 - Being Organised

Being organised in your pursuit of building power can actually be seen as dangerous, because society is set up to keep people in organised chaos. When you're organised and structured, especially if that same mindset spreads to the people you're building with, it becomes a real threat to the system. There's nothing more powerful than a group of people who are organised and ready for action.

If you want to be successful in building power, being organised shows that you have order and structure, and that makes people take you seriously.

#2 - Live Your Life with Discipline

Building power requires a lot of discipline, and without it, you'll struggle to get anywhere. This is one of the qualities that makes you dangerous. There's nothing more dangerous than someone who is relentless and highly disciplined when it comes to their mission. A person with that level of focus becomes hard to stop.

When you move with discipline, it's hard for anyone to distract or derail you. Your dedication keeps you on track, while most people today can't even stick to their basic daily routine. So I say this being disciplined in today's world can be seen as dangerous, especially when you're using that discipline with a clear purpose to build real power.

#3 - Being Connected to the People

On your path to building power, it's important to stay connected to the people you're building with. There's nothing more powerful than someone who truly understands the everyday person. When you're connected to the real issues people face, and you're grounded in their everyday struggles, you become someone they can trust.

That kind of connection builds influence, and influence builds power, because people are more likely to follow someone who genuinely understands their pain and is committed to leading them toward something better.

#4 - Awareness of Your Own Power

In your pursuit of building power, you must have awareness of your own power. Being aware of it gives you better control over how you use it. If you lack that awareness, you could end up causing problems simply because you don't fully understand the power you hold. It's important to assess how your power affects those around you especially the people you're building with. That level of awareness helps prevent the misuse or abuse of power, knowing just how much damage it could cause if handled recklessly.

#5 - Building Power with Purpose

There's nothing more powerful than building with purpose. When your rise to power is backed by purpose, it brings deeper meaning and substance to everything you do. Without purpose, it's easy to misuse or waste the power you gain, because there's no clear direction. Purpose gives your power structure, focus, and intention. Without it, you're just moving with no real goal, and that defeats the whole point of building power in the first place.

Measuring Trust

When building power, you're going to have to trust people. And I get it, we live in a time where trust is rare. So the question becomes, how do you measure trust in those you're working with? The best way is to mirror the trust they show you. Give them back the same level of trust they give you, nothing more, nothing less.

Also, understand that trust has to be measured again and again over time. People change. Sometimes life changes people's situations, which then affects their behaviour or mindset. That's why it's important to keep assessing how much you can trust someone as you go. Learning how to measure trust is a skill you gain through experience, by watching how people show up, how they handle pressure, and how they treat others around them.

Don't Let People Know Your Every Move

When building power, it's important to be very strategic. That means not letting everyone know what your next move is. If people know your every move, you make it easy for them to anticipate your steps, and that's not wise. Understand that not everyone around you has your best interests at heart. Not everyone wants to see you succeed in building power. Some may even try to sabotage you, whether directly or indirectly.

Be careful who you share your plans with. Remember, it's not the outsiders you need to worry about, they usually don't know much about you. It's the ones closest to you, the ones who already have access to personal information, that you really need to keep an eye on.

M.O.E (Mission Over Everything)

When putting the Mission Over Everything, we need to understand how this mindset really works. What it means is that you must be willing to put the mission above your own feelings, your ego, and even your personal wants. Some people might not agree with the idea of putting the mission before their emotions, and that's understandable. But we have to realise that feelings are temporary, they come and go. What you don't want is for your emotions to get in the way of your mission to build power. Feelings can cloud your judgement, because they don't run on logic.

To become one of the most dangerous people, you have to make the mission your top priority, no matter what. You can't let anything or anyone stand in your way. When you operate with the Mission Over Everything mindset, it means you're ready to do whatever it takes to reach your goal of building power. That's what this mission is about.

Some may ask, what does it really mean to live by the M.O.E mindset? Let's break down the philosophy with a few key principles:

#1 - Logic Over Emotions

On your journey to building power, you need to operate with logic and make sure it overrides your emotions. I understand some people will argue and say, "We're only human," or "It's natural to be emotional sometimes," which is true, we're not robots. But building power requires decisions that come from a rational, logical place. Emotional and erratic behaviour has no place when you're trying to build power. So if you're someone who struggles with emotional instability or finds it hard to keep your emotions balanced, that's something you need to work on before you fully commit to building power.

#2 - Be Willing to Distance Yourself from Those Who Will Hinder You from Completing the Mission

Completing the mission is one of the most important parts of building power. You must be willing to distance yourself from anyone who could hold you back, even if they're people you're close to. I understand this isn't easy. No one wants to push away their close friends or loved ones. But building power with purpose will require some tough sacrifices. These decisions can either make or break you. You'll have to choose: are you going to keep people around who slow you down, or will you cut ties so that your mission can move forward? The choice is yours.

#3 - To Be Intolerant to Ignorance

As you build power, you need to have a personal policy that you also encourage among your team, that ignorance will not be tolerated. This doesn't mean looking down on people who lack knowledge. We're all learning and growing at different paces. But it does mean that people shouldn't remain stuck in their ignorance.

Ignorance is harming a lot of people in today's world. Some people don't even realise they're operating from a place of ignorance until someone points it out. And even when they do become aware, many still refuse to change. That kind of mindset can spread like a virus, and it serves no good purpose.

This is why you must enforce a no-ignorance mindset with those around you. Promote awareness and growth as a way of life. If anyone in your circle breaks this standard, they should only be given a few chances to turn it around. When building power, ignorance can't be allowed to grow, it will slow your progress and possibly destroy everything you're working for.

#4 - A No-Nonsense Attitude

Another ingredient to the M.O.E philosophy is having a no-nonsense attitude. Building power will require you to move with this type of mindset because it's exactly what's needed in today's world. We live in a social media era where a lot of nonsense is being pushed online to distract people and keep them from making real progress. Every day, pointless trends and shallow agendas flood people's screens, keeping them in a state of confusion and chaos. This makes it harder for revolutionary voices with real substance to reach the people.

To fight back against the nonsense and distraction that society throws at us, you must be willing to operate with a no-nonsense attitude, or at least be open to developing one as you go. The purpose of this attitude is to reinforce a focused, direct, and serious approach to life. It's about being clear and straight to the point when getting things done.

This mindset needs to be part of the M.O.E philosophy because it shows people that you're serious. You're not here to play games or entertain foolishness. It shows you won't tolerate childish behaviour if it ever presents itself, and that you're not someone who deals in fantasy. The no-nonsense attitude is grounded in reality, and anything that's not realistic or practical be quickly dismissed.

#5 - Understanding the Mission Is Not Singular

The mission to build power is not just about you. It's not for selfish gain. The mission is meant to serve a bigger purpose, not just for your own life, but for others too, with the goal of creating a better future.

What this really means is that anyone who chooses to join you on the journey of building power becomes part of the mission. This is something both you and the people with you must fully understand. Be aware, though, not everyone will get this. Some people have selfish minds and hearts, and because of that, they may look down on you or criticise your efforts.

You also have to realise that not everyone's mindset is built to understand this way of thinking. We live in a modern-day society where a lot of people are still mentally stuck. Their mindset hasn't grown past what they were taught by the system, by school, by mainstream media, and by the Babylon structure itself. Many are still thinking in basic, narrow ways. So the idea that the mission isn't just about one person might go over some people's heads.

But don't let that discourage you. Stick to this philosophy. Over time, as people's thinking evolves and more start to see the bigger picture, the idea of collective power and purpose will begin to make sense. Revolutionary thinking will spread, and with it, the understanding that the mission is for everyone.

Chapter 8

―――

Compete For People

When building power, you must understand that you have to be willing to put yourself in a competitor's position. You won't be taken seriously if you're not seen as someone the opposition can actually compete with. On the journey of building power, whether you realise it or not, you are competing for the partnership of people who can join forces with you to help you build. As a competitor, you're competing for the following:

#1 - Attention of the people

As a competitor for power, you'll be fighting for the attention of the people. You need their attention so you can bring them on board to help contribute to the building process. Once you have their attention with good intentions and something valuable to offer, that's what I call valuable attention, because you've earned it through substance and purpose, not empty noise. You used that attention to create something meaningful.

#2 - The Minds of the people

Winning the minds of the people is just as important. Once you've got their attention, the next step is to help them think differently. The aim is to revolutionise their minds so they become power-focused, shifting from basic thinking to a higher level that aligns with the mission of building power. Competing for the minds of the people is about influence, helping them to see the bigger picture and encouraging them to support your vision of change.

But let me say this: if you manage to gain the minds of the people, do not abuse that power. If you do, it will backfire on you eventually. Misusing that influence will strip you of the very power you worked so hard to build.

#3 - The Trust of the People

On your journey to building power, you will have to compete for the trust of the people if you want them to build with you. This process can take time, so you'll need to be patient. We live in a world where trust is constantly being abused by politicians, police, religious leaders, online influencers, and more. Because of this, most people today struggle to trust others, which makes this part of the journey more difficult.

So how do you earn trust in a world filled with distrust? The answer is consistency. You must be consistent in the character you show to people. If your actions don't match what you claim to be about, people will start to notice. They'll see the inconsistency and begin to challenge it, and that could lead to resistance. If the people don't trust you, they won't follow you.

#4 - For the Participation of the People

To be a strong competitor, you'll also need to compete for the participation of the people. Without their participation, it will be hard, if not impossible, to build power. Of course, you can influence people as an individual, but if you're serious about growing your influence and impact, you'll need people behind you.

The more people you have participating in the power-building process, the stronger your movement becomes. The goal here is to get as many people involved as possible so that your strength multiplies. It's not about control, it's about unity, collaboration, and shared purpose.

#5 - The Time of the People

As a competitor, you'll also be competing for people's time. That means you need to get people to willingly give their time to your revolutionary mission of building power. This isn't easy. People today are constantly distracted and pulled in many different directions; from social media to work, entertainment, and personal struggles.

If you want their time, you need to bring something valuable to the table. People don't want to feel like their time is being wasted. So whatever you're offering them, make sure it's worth their energy, their effort, and their trust.

Chapter 9

Power From Within

When building power in today's society, you must first understand where true, organic power comes from. If you spend your time searching for power outside of yourself, you're already missing the point. The power you're looking for is already inside you. The problem is, you might not be aware of it or know how to activate it.

The best way to discover the power within is to challenge yourself with things that may seem impossible at first, but are actually doable if you put your mind to it. Many people make the mistake of always looking outside themselves. That's what we call seeking validation. But if you truly want to build power, start by looking inward

Patience During the Power-Building Process

When you're building power among the people, patience is key. This is not a quick fix. It takes time, sometimes years, to build the level of power you're aiming for. You have to allow people time to adjust to the philosophy or ideas you're trying to build with.

Patience is powerful. Without it, you'll end up making rushed decisions that could have been avoided if you just waited a bit longer. Understand this is a long journey, not an overnight process. There will be delays. Things will come up that you can't control. Those moments will test your patience and reveal how committed you really are. Will you keep going? Or will you fold under pressure?

Build Power with Caution, Not Paranoia

To succeed in building power, you need to approach the process with caution, but not paranoia. Trying to build power while living in a paranoid state will only hold you back.

In a society where trust is rare, it's easy to understand why many people walk around guarded, especially if they've been betrayed by people close to them. That kind of pain can leave deep scars. But when you're building power, you have to take a different approach. You must set aside personal trauma and adopt a more logical and balanced mindset.

This isn't a solo mission. Building real power requires support from others. That means learning to trust, even if it's not easy. No, you shouldn't trust everyone, that's not wise. But building power without trust is nearly impossible.

You'll have a better chance of success when you build with a group, rather than trying to do it all on your own. Alone, you're an easy target. Together, you're a powerful force. Just make sure you move with caution, use discernment, so you can spot the ones who aren't trustworthy along the way.

Be Bold in Your Claim for Power

Building power takes boldness. Claiming power is not for the shy or the timid. You have to be willing to step out into the world and make your intentions known. When you're claiming power, it's not something you ask for, it's something you take. Be ready to take power into your own hands. Make sure the power you're reaching for is yours, not someone else's. Be bold enough to exercise that power, but always do it with caution.

If you're serious about claiming power, you have to take a stand and refuse to back down, no matter the backlash or pressure that may come your way. Say what you mean, mean what you say, and own your claim to power without apology. Understand this: we live in a society that would rather see you stuck at the bottom, settling for a life of mediocrity. So it's on you to rise up and claim your power with force, because no one else is going to hand it to you.

Use Rejection to Fuel Your Power from Within

Building power isn't easy. You'll need real resilience and strength for this journey. One thing you're guaranteed to face along the way is rejection. And it won't always feel good. Some people won't believe you can do what you're setting out to do. Others might reject your invitation to join the mission. And many people, especially in a society like Babylon, are too caught up in survival mode to even think about building anything greater.

But don't let rejection discourage you. Don't let it be the reason you give up. Instead, let rejection fuel your fire. Use it to push your mission harder. Yes, it's tough, especially when rejection comes from people you respect or care about. But don't see it as failure. See it as redirection. Use it to sharpen your strategy and find the right people who are ready to join forces with you. Be persistent. Lock in a winner's mindset. Stay focused on your goal with relentless determination. That's how you build real power.

Act Upon Your Revolutionary Thinking

One of the most important keys to building power is to act on your revolutionary thinking. Having a revolutionary mindset is great, but thinking alone is not enough. At some point, you have to move. You have to take action. You have to bring those bold ideas to life.

This is where most people fall off. They talk a good talk but freeze when it's time to act. Why? Because action requires effort. It demands change. And stepping into the unknown can be scary. But if you don't act on your ideas, the whole power-building process falls apart. Think of action as the fuel that keeps the engine running. Without it, nothing moves.

If you want to see your vision come alive, stop holding back. Stop overthinking. Stop waiting for the perfect moment. Start acting on what you believe. That's the only way real change and real power is built.

Be Prepared to Deal with Character Assassination

On your journey to building power, there are serious consequences that come with the territory, one of them is character assassination. This is a tactic used to attack your name and reputation with the aim of breaking you down bit by bit. For example, if your power and influence begin to pose a threat to the government, they may use a first-line defence tactic; character assassination. They'll often use the media to dig up anything they can find online to damage your image, without having to get directly involved. That's why I mentioned earlier the importance of watching what you post online. It can easily be used against you in the future.

But it's not just governments or the media. Character assassination can come from anyone who doesn't want to see you rise. It could be enemies, rivals, or even people you once trusted. You need to be ready for this. The best way to handle these attacks is often to stay silent. Some people may disagree, but ask yourself: why waste your energy responding to false accusations you know aren't true? Isn't your energy better spent focusing on your mission? Stay locked in on your purpose. Only respond if it becomes absolutely necessary otherwise, let your actions speak louder than their words.

Aim to Spread Your Building Power Philosophy Worldwide

When building power, it's important to think globally. Spreading your philosophy around the world isn't about chasing fame or becoming popular, it's about helping to uplift people beyond your immediate surroundings. The reality is, being at the bottom of society is not just a local issue. It's a global problem. All around the world, governments are hoarding resources and giving people only the crumbs. This isn't just happening in the West, it's happening everywhere.

So, the goal of spreading this philosophy is to reach communities across the world that are crying out for real change. People need to reclaim their power. They need to understand they can take control of their future. When you spread this philosophy globally, you help plant seeds of change in different places. You help others build power in their own corners of the world, not just for themselves, but for the next generation too. This is about starting a movement that builds better futures worldwide.

Create a Revolutionary Coalition While Building Power

On your journey to building power, one of the best things you can do is form a revolutionary group coalition. For those who may not know what that means, let me explain briefly. A revolutionary coalition is a group of people who come together to stand against the imbalance of power in society, with the goal of bringing power back to the everyday person, the ones often left out or pushed to the bottom.

As I've said before, building power is not a solo mission. Yes, it might start with just one person who has a powerful revolutionary blueprint they want to share with the world. But if you want to maintain that power in the long term, you'll need to work with others. You'll need to unite with like-minded individuals who share the same values and vision. Everyone in the coalition should be committed to contributing their skills, energy, and ideas to help push the power-building process forward.

Let's look at some steps you can take to begin forming this kind of coalition:

#1 - Build Ally-Like Relationships With People Who Show Interest in Your Philosophy

On your journey to building power, you may come across people who take a real interest in your philosophy. This can be an important time to keep those people engaged by building strong, ally-like relationships with them. To succeed at this, your philosophy needs to keep evolving in a way that helps guide people in the right direction, a direction that brings real value and long-term benefits to their lives.

#2 - Accept Podcast Invitations That Allow You to Share Your Message

In today's world, where podcasts are popular across social media platforms like YouTube, it's a smart move to take advantage of these platforms to spread your philosophy to a wider audience. Doing this can expose you to new people who may want to join your power-building journey. Most podcasters are focused on promoting their content, which works in your favour as it helps get your message seen and heard by even more people across different platforms.

#3 - Engage Followers of Your Philosophy Into Active Participants

When you're building power with a working philosophy, you may start gaining followers, especially if you have a social media platform like Facebook or Instagram. That's the era we live in now. But when you're spreading a meaningful philosophy across society, it's not enough for people to just follow you online.

Let's be honest, a lot of social media followers only watch and scroll. If they like your content, they might watch every video you post. That's not a bad thing, but the goal is to get your followers to go beyond just watching. You want to turn them into active participants who help you build power.

To do that, you need a solid, working foundation, something they can actually be part of. Without it, they'll remain passive, and you'll miss the opportunity to build something bigger.

Here are some things to think about as you turn your followers into active participants:

- What kind of participation do you want from them?

- How will you engage them in practical ways?

- What benefits will they get from being actively involved?

#4 - Create a Revolutionary Foundation for People to Participate In

As mentioned earlier, if you want your followers to help you build power, you need to create a revolutionary foundation for them to participate in. Without it, people will have nothing to connect with or work toward. Eventually, they'll fade away, and you'll be back at square one, trying to rebuild from scratch.

While creating this foundation, keep these key points in mind:

- What are the current needs of the people?

- What kind of services or support will truly benefit them?

- Can you build a strong and respectable foundation rooted in principles and morals that people can align with?

Test Your Theory Before You Roll It Out to Society

When building power with people, it's important to test your theories first to see what works and what doesn't. The reason you want to test your philosophical theory before sharing it widely is because you need to make sure it will actually have a positive effect on the people, especially those you're trying to build with.

Make sure your theory has been tested and has real evidence that it works. That way, when you present it to others, you can show them proof and help them understand how to apply it in their own lives.

It's not wise to roll out a theory that hasn't been tested or lived through. Doing so can actually be harmful and create more confusion in a society that's already full of chaos. If you truly want to make an impact, roll out your philosophy with caution, proper planning, and a clear idea of how it will work in real life.

Chapter 10

Break The Matrix

First, let's talk about what the matrix is so we can understand what it means. The matrix is an illusion, an imaginary version of reality placed over the everyday person and accepted as normal. From childhood to adulthood, this illusion is pushed on you so hard that most people end up fully accepting it. Once that happens, they become heavily conditioned, passive, and easy to control. This is done on purpose to keep people from stepping out of line or rebelling against the system.

If you're serious about building power, you must be willing to opt out of the matrix. That means going against what society expects or tells you is normal. Following the crowd will only keep you stuck in the same spot. You have to be brave enough to go against the grain if you really want to rise.

Some may ask, how do you opt out of the matrix when your whole life has been shaped by it? Let's look at how you can start breaking free from this illusion:

#1 - Define your life through your own lens

When you choose to step out of the matrix, the first thing you must do is define your life through your own lens, without any outside control. Especially in today's Western society, where things feel chaotic and most people are just doing random things with no real direction. That's why you have to take charge of your own life and be clear about what you want from it. Be careful not to let someone else define your path for you. Building power comes from creating your own definition of life, with your own rules and boundaries, rules that don't come from the matrix that most people are trapped in.

#2 - Put up resistance against societal indoctrination

Choosing to step out of the matrix also means you'll need to put up strong resistance against societal indoctrination. You might ask, what does that even mean? Societal indoctrination is when people are told how to live, what to follow, and how to think without ever thinking for themselves. It's like being stuck in a mental trance.

That's why it's so important to push back against this if you're serious about building your own power. But before you do, ask yourself if you're truly ready to take that step. Once you go all in, there's no turning back to the old way of life. That mediocre lifestyle you once lived will no longer exist, it dies the moment you choose a new path. And that new path comes with higher standards and a new way of living. So take your time, think it through, and make sure you're ready before you fully commit to this journey of resistance.

#3 - Don't allow yourself to be dictated to

Stepping out of the matrix isn't easy for most people, especially in today's world where many of us are born into a system that tells us how to think and live. Breaking free from that system takes strength, defiance, self-belief, and a mix of other inner qualities. But it's possible. To break away from this kind of control, you must become the one who directs your own life. The idea behind this philosophy is to keep the control and pressure of society as far away from you as possible. Don't let the system define your life in any way. Resist the control of society in every way you can, especially, if you're serious about stepping out of the matrix.

#4 - Stand by your own principles and philosophy even if society rejects them

If you're going to opt out of the matrix, you have to stand by your own principles and beliefs, even if society doesn't agree with them. This is where your character will be tested. Are you truly committed to your philosophy, or will you bend under pressure when people push back? The rejection you might face can come from ignorance, fear, or just people not understanding your perspective. But that doesn't mean you should let go of what you believe. If you're serious about breaking free from the matrix, then you must stand firm in what you represent, no matter how unpopular it might be.

Chapter 11

—-

Take Power Now

On your journey to building power, your work ethic has to be at a high standard. The amount of work you put in will determine the results you get. If your work ethic is anything less than relentless, your rise to power will be delayed and may take longer than necessary. For example, if you're doing an online course that's self-paced, you can't really say how long it will take to finish. That all depends on how much time and effort you put into it. Building power works the same way. The difference is, if you're starting from scratch, meaning you're coming from the bottom of society, it may take years to reach your goal, so patience is going to be key.

Some people may ask what it really means to have a relentless work ethic. Let's look at what that might look like in today's modern western society. For example, if you're the kind of person that just goes to work, comes home, watches a bit of TV, Netflix or Amazon Prime, and then goes to bed only to repeat the same routine every day, then you're likely to stay in the same spot with little or no progress. You'll need to put in extra work outside your 9-5 hours if you want to speed up your journey to building power. I'm not talking about doing overtime at your job. I'm talking about investing time into yourself.

You need to spend at least one hour each weekday on building yourself up for power. For some people, the weekend might be for rest or going out to party. But if you're serious about building power with a relentless work ethic, you may need to give up some of that partying or chilling time and use it to work on your goals. For most people in society today, that kind of sacrifice doesn't sound appealing, because we live in a world that thrives on entertainment. But if you truly want to take power back into your own hands, you'll need to build a disciplined, military-style work ethic. Anything less than that just won't be enough to reach the top levels of power.

Always keep an eye on your power structure

One of the biggest mistakes you can make when building your power structure is to leave it unattended. It's in your best interest to keep an eye on it and make sure your operation is running how it's supposed to. A common issue in many western workplaces is that the owner hardly ever shows up to see how things are going. They hire managers and supervisors to handle the day-to-day running of the business, but in many cases, these managers can run it into the ground because they lack the proper skills to maintain a smooth and effective work environment.

Once you start building your power structure, you'll likely have certain values and principles about how you want things to operate. So even if you put someone else in charge of a section, it's still important to check in and make sure things are being handled the right way. The reason I say this is because, as your operation grows and more people join your mission, there's a higher chance of internal conflict. Different people bring different personalities and ways of thinking, and when those clash, it can lead to problems that might harm the structure you've built. Keeping an eye on things helps you step in early and prevent those issues from getting worse.

Outmanoeuvre your competitors in power

As you rise in power, understand that you're going to be competing with others who are already in power. In today's world, many of those in control are using greed, lies, distraction, and manipulation to keep their grip on the people. This has been their strategy for years. If you want to get the people's attention and win their trust, you'll need to create a plan and strategy that allows you to outmanoeuvre your competitors. Keep in mind, your competition is not playing fair, so don't expect the process to be smooth. You may have to get your hands a little dirty, just make sure you're still moving with purpose and not losing your integrity.

Let's now explore some ways you can go about outmanoeuvring the competition in power:

#1 - Study your competitor

Studying your competitor is necessary because you need to understand what you're up against. Without knowing anything about your competitor in power, you won't be able to compete or reach their level. Studying your competitor helps you gather the information you can use as a tool to compete more effectively.

#2 - Study your competitor's strengths and weaknesses

It's important to look at both the strengths and weaknesses of your competitor. This is a smart strategy to help you outmanoeuvre them. When you know what they're good at and where they fall short, you can figure out what you need to do better in order to take your own power to the next level.

#3 - Study how your competitor operates

You need to study how your competitor operates if you're serious about building power. Every competitor has a unique way of doing things to achieve their goals. When you understand how they work, you can see what kind of impact their actions have on society, whether good or bad. This gives you the chance to learn what to do and what not to do so you can use your power more effectively. Studying your competitors helps you improve your own strategies, which can give you the edge to eventually surpass them.

#4 - Use your findings to outmanoeuvre them

As you pursue power, once you've gathered enough information about your competitors, it's time to use that knowledge to outsmart and outmanoeuvre them. This doesn't mean playing dirty or creating chaos, it simply means using what you've learned as a resource to get ahead. Let your strategy and preparation speak for you. Nothing more, nothing less.

Don't tear down others in order to build power

When building power, don't get caught up in tearing others down. That's not the right way to build. If you move with that kind of destructive mindset, your success won't last long. You'll only create more enemies, and people like that can't be trusted, they'll turn on anyone just to get ahead.

Building power isn't about crushing everyone around you. It's about empowering yourself and others so you all tap into your inner strength and take action to make your time on this earth count. That's real power.

Don't show vulnerability in the public eye

Building power takes strength, focus, and a serious will to win. What you don't want to do is show your vulnerability in front of the public. Some people may not agree with this and say it's unhealthy to keep your feelings to yourself, especially if you're struggling inside.

Let me be clear, I'm not saying you should act like a robot. We're human, and feelings are real. But we also have to be honest: this society doesn't always show compassion.

We've all seen people post videos online crying about something serious that broke them down, and days later, they're the butt of jokes, memes, and mockery. In a world like this, where people prey on weakness, showing public vulnerability can be dangerous. It can be used to manipulate, control, or destroy you.

That's why, when building power, you need to stay strong in public and keep your weak moments private. Find safe spaces where you can let it out, but the public eye, especially on social media, doesn't need to see that side of you.

Take power into your own hands

If you want power, you have to take it. Nobody, especially not society or the government, is going to hand it over to you. You're not automatically entitled to power just because you want it.

You've got to claim it for yourself. Use your inner strength to go after what you need and put that power to work for your mission. Own it. Live it. Move with purpose.

Don't Be Afraid to Exercise Your Power

Building power means that at some point, you'll have to use it. You must show what your power can do and how it can inspire others to take action in their own lives. Don't be afraid to exercise your power. If fear holds you back, you'll never discover the full impact you're capable of.

That fear will trap you in a powerless state, frustrated, restless, and stuck. It's like locking yourself in a prison and throwing away the key.

But when you start using your power, you begin to understand what you're truly capable of. You learn how to control it, manage it, and master it. You see both the strengths and weaknesses your power holds, and that's exactly why you must use it boldly and without hesitation.

Dictate Your Own Freedom

To build power, you must take full control of your own freedom, by any means necessary. Don't let anyone else decide what freedom should look like for you.

In Western society, silent dictatorship is everywhere. The government uses laws and hidden tactics to shape how people live, without openly saying it. Most people don't even realise how much they've been controlled, and as a result, they find it hard to break free.

But when you dictate your own freedom, you take your

power back. You decide how you want to live, on your own terms, not theirs.

This kind of declaration is bold. It's a real act of self-empowerment. And it's one of the most powerful moves you can make on your journey to lasting power.

Power Does Not Require Anybody's Approval

If you're truly serious about building power, understand this: your power doesn't need anyone's approval but your own.

If you spend your time trying to get everyone's approval, you'll stay stuck. Not everyone will see the world through your lens. Not everyone will understand your mission, and that's okay.

Seeking approval from people who don't even understand your vision is a waste of energy Worse, it shows a lack of belief in yourself. Real power starts from within. Approve of yourself. Believe in your purpose That's the only green light you need to rise.

Chapter 12

Master or Slave

When building power, we must understand why the majority of people in everyday society remain powerless, while a small percentage hold most of the power.

This fundamental question strikes at the heart of human civilisation and reveals one of the most uncomfortable truths about our world. If you look around, you'll notice that power is not distributed equally among people. It never has been, and it never will be. This isn't an accident or some cosmic mistake, it's the result of specific mindsets, behaviours, and choices that separate those who rise to positions of influence from those who remain trapped in cycles of dependency and mediocrity.

The truth is, most people are conditioned from birth to accept powerlessness as their natural state. They're taught to follow rules without question, to seek permission before acting, and to believe that their circumstances are beyond their control. This conditioning runs so deep that many don't even recognise they're living as mental slaves, bound by invisible chains of limitation that society has placed on their minds.

In modern-day Babylon, the system is specifically designed to keep the masses powerless while concentrating control in the hands of a few. The education system teaches compliance, not critical thinking. The media feeds people entertainment and distractions instead of empowering knowledge. The economic structure creates dependency on jobs and government assistance rather than encouraging true independence and wealth creation. Every institution works together to maintain this power imbalance, ensuring that the majority remain consumers and followers rather than creators and leaders.

The Slave

The slave doesn't demand power, they beg for what they want, hoping that one day a miracle will come. The slave takes no real action toward power. They moan and complain about life's difficulties and what they don't have. The slave becomes envious of those who are successful but has no idea of the sacrifices those people made to reach that level.

The slave settles for a life of mediocrity. They play it safe, trapped by self-doubt and fear of stepping out of their comfort zone to succeed beyond what society expects. They don't dictate their own life but instead accept whatever society hands them, without question. They stay stuck in a prison of mental indoctrination.

The slave is ignorant, refuses to read or learn, and avoids educating themselves. This lack of knowledge keeps them powerless and easily manipulated by those in control.

The Master

The master doesn't just demand power, they take it. They don't wait around or ask for permission. They don't believe in hoping for miracles. Instead, the master creates a plan, takes action, and stays focused on getting results.

The master is willing to make the necessary sacrifices to achieve their goals. In their mind, excuses are unacceptable. Excuses are seen as a weak way to avoid doing what must be done.

The master takes power into their own hands without apology. What people say, think, or feel does not matter to them. They reject a mediocre life, which is why they don't follow the same path as society.

The master governs their own life. They aren't interested in what society says they should be. They lead their own thoughts, their own vision, and follow their own direction, free from outside influence.

The master is more than ready to step outside the comfort zone to reach higher levels of success. They're not afraid of the challenges that come with it, because they expect it.

Most importantly, the master is always hungry for knowledge. They keep learning and growing, which gives them a clear advantage over those who choose to stay uninformed. This mindset is what keeps the master ahead, and in power.

Conclusion

The conclusion drawn from comparing the master and the slave is this, you cannot build power with the mindset of a slave. You must take on the mentality of a master. The master and the slave are two completely different people with two completely different ways of thinking. One sits back, waits, and hopes life will somehow deliver a miracle. The other gets up, moves boldly, and takes control of life to create the results they want.

To build real power, you have to create your own opportunities. You have to be willing to step away from the comfort of mediocrity and do what most people won't. You must be ready to get your hands dirty if that's what it takes. That means pushing beyond what society expects of you and breaking through the invisible limits it tries to place on you. Building power requires a level of relentlessness that will drive you far beyond the ordinary pace of life.

This is what it means to build power, to move without fear, to break boundaries, and to believe there is no limit to what you can achieve if you have the right mindset, the right attitude, and the resilience to keep going no matter what.

Chapter 13

——

Think Freely Always

In modern-day Babylon, most people don't truly understand the responsibility that comes with power. That's because many have never experienced what real power feels like or looks like in everyday life. Most people only know a lifestyle built on survival, settling for the crumbs the government hands out. They've grown used to being powerless, and if they ever do come into any form of power, there's a high chance they'll misuse it and end up becoming the enemy of the people.

This is why it's so important to understand how to use the power you have. You can't let it control you. You must be the one in full control of the power, not the other way around.

The core idea here is to become the people's champion. Your mission in building power must be to work with the people, not against them, even if they think differently from you or see things in another way. The goal is to find common ground and figure out how to get things done together, despite differences in personality or character.

Now, being the people's champion doesn't mean everyone is going to like your decisions. It doesn't mean you'll always keep people happy, because that's not realistic. You'll have to make tough decisions that support the bigger picture and the mission you've set out to accomplish. Some people will disagree with you. Some will struggle to understand your vision. Some won't be able to see beyond the present moment to recognise the long-term goal. These challenges are normal in the process of building power.

To stay on solid ground with the people you're building with, your aim should be to avoid being at odds with the majority. Don't get distracted by the few who don't agree with you. Focus on the bigger picture, making sure the majority are with you is what matters most.

Never let the power get to your head. Stay grounded. Always remember that the people who support your mission are long-term allies and without them, your journey to power can't be fulfilled.

Think Like a Free Person

If you want to build power, one of the first things you need to master is your own mind, free from the influence of the western narrative. To truly succeed in building power, you must think like a free person.

This means refusing to think like a slave. You need to allow your thoughts to flow freely, outside of the average way society wants you to think. It's crucial that you learn how to think outside the box, because that's the level of thinking it takes to build real power. Rising to power has no room for small or limited thinking. That's the same mindset that keeps many people stuck in a powerless state.

Now, I get it. For most people, especially those living in survival mode every day, thinking freely can feel almost impossible, especially when you don't have access to the right knowledge. So, how do you break free and start thinking like a free person in a society that's designed to keep your mind locked in a mental prison?

Let's break it down with a few steps to help you begin shifting your mindset and stepping into your power:

#1 - Engage in Research

One of the key parts of thinking like a free person is doing your own research. This helps you find out the truth for yourself instead of just accepting what someone else tells you. There's real power in discovering things on your own.

When you blindly take in information without checking it for yourself, you give someone else control over what you believe. They now have power over you. But when you do your own research, the power shifts back into your hands. It gives you more control over the information you take in, and that control is everything.

#2 - Remain a Student of Life No Matter How Much You Know

A big part of gaining power is staying a student of life, no matter how much knowledge you already have. Power doesn't just come from what you know, it comes from how you apply what you know.

So ask yourself: if power comes from using the knowledge you gain, wouldn't it make sense to keep learning?

Always stay open to learning more. That mindset keeps you growing.

#3 - Form Your Own Non-Societal Opinions

To build power, you need to have your own opinions, ones that aren't shaped by society's rules. Forming your own opinions means you have a mind of your own. That alone is power.

Owning your mind puts you in control of your own story. You're not boxed in by what society thinks or expects. Building power means breaking through limits that have been put on you. It means reaching for levels of success you once thought were out of your reach.

When you form your own opinions, you open the door to new ways of thinking. And those new ways can take your life to the next level and support your journey of building real power.

#4 - Develop Your Own Philosophy

If you're serious about building power, you need to develop your own philosophy. This means creating your own set of beliefs, values, and ideas that guide how you live and make decisions.

Having your own philosophy brings you power, and it helps you influence others too. The more people who connect with your philosophy, the more respect and influence you gain.

With influence comes action. You can now use your power to inspire others to move with you, especially if your mission is to create real change.

The key message here is this: the moment you take full ownership of your own philosophy, you step into a position of power. You're no longer controlled or easily manipulated. You are in control of how you live your life.

Use Technology as a Tool to Build Power

Now that we live in a technological era with access to the internet, it would be wise to use it as a tool to build power. Some people say the internet is a gift and a curse, and that might be true to an extent. But it's only a curse if you're not using it with purpose. If you use technology to empower yourself and level up, then it can work in your favour.

If you're on a journey to build power, you can use social media platforms to spread your influence online. Technology gives you a chance to move forward in life, and it plays a huge role in today's modern world. Social media is a great tool to run ad campaigns, promote your business, or share your message through a social media page. It also allows you to connect with people across the world, which can be very powerful, if used properly.

Technology won't benefit you if all you focus on is the negative side of it. There's good and bad in everything. What matters is how you choose to use it. Use it wisely and take advantage of everything it offers to help move your power-building journey forward.

Be Self-Governed

Another strong way to build power in today's western world is to be self-governed. The ability to govern yourself is something the government doesn't want people to experience. Why? Because if people could govern themselves, there would be no need to rely on the system, and that would weaken the government's control.

The system is set up to make you depend on it. That's how they maintain power. But when you become self-governed, you take that power back into your own hands. You gain more control over how you live your life and how you make decisions.

Being self-governed cuts off any form of forced dictatorship coming your way. It gives you the freedom to live on your own terms, and that's real power.

Not Every Battle Needs to Be Fought

There is real power in knowing that not every battle in life needs to be fought. Think about it, if you tried to fight every single battle that came your way, you'd wear yourself out. That's why it's important to know when to step back and surrender, not out of weakness, but as a smart strategy to conserve your power.

Imagine being at war with an opposing army that outnumbers you. Wouldn't it be wiser to retreat, regroup, and bring in reinforcements instead of charging in and losing everything?

Some battles can't be won, no matter how hard you try. And that's okay.

The strength in this mindset comes from acceptance, knowing when to surrender and save your energy for the battles that truly matter.

The Revolution Only Works for Those Who Participate

Building power is a revolutionary act that brings about change, whether good or bad. Either way, it's a powerful force for transformation.

If you're someone who wants to see change in your life, then you must be a participant in that change. True power comes from being involved in your own revolution. The revolution won't help you if you're just sitting around waiting for someone else to do what you could do for yourself. It doesn't support passivity. It demands action.

If you believe you can sit back and enjoy the benefits of someone else's hard work, you're in for a rude awakening. Power doesn't come from watching others, it comes from showing up, putting in the work, and being part of the movement.

If the years have gone by and your life still looks the same, ask yourself: what have I actually done to bring about change? What part have I played in my own revolution?

Those who understand that power comes through sacrifice also understand that participation is vital. But those who refuse to take part in their own transformation will keep suffering under the weight of modern-day society and government control.

Chapter 14

Know When To Strike

On your rise to building power, it's important to know and understand when to strike. What I mean by this is that you don't want to show or use your power too early when it's not needed. We live in a very impulsive society where most people act on emotion without thinking things through.

On your journey to power, you'll always face opposers, people who will push back no matter what. That's just part of the price you pay when building power. Knowing the right time to strike back is key. Those who react without strategy often end up destroying themselves.

You must strike when your opposition least expects it. Be calculated and strategic. Make sure every move you make has weight and real impact. And when I say "strike," I don't mean using violence. What I'm talking about is acting with intent, taking your next step with precision and purpose.

Be Willing to Invest in the Cost of Building Power

Building power comes with a cost. It's not free. If you're serious about building power, you'll have to be willing to invest, whether that's your money, your time, your effort, or your energy.

If you're not prepared to invest in the cost of building power, then you can't expect real progress. The willingness to invest is what fuels your growth. It's what helps you upgrade your life on your own terms, without limits.

Investing in your power is a decision, and it's one you must make if you want to rise.

Surrender to the Rhythm of Existence

In order to build power, you will need to surrender to the rhythm of existence. What I mean by this is that you can't keep fighting the natural direction your life is heading. Trying to resist it will only bring chaos within yourself.

You need to understand that life will change direction from time to time. Circumstances and events will come that force you to shift how you live, and all of that is part of the rhythm of your life. Since this is about building power, let's relate it to that journey.

As you rise to power, you'll feel the impact of that journey in every part of your life. Once you decide to start this path, many things will change. Your personal life will shift. Your thinking will shift. I like to call this the *rhythm of changes*, because life has its own natural rhythm that none of us can control.

Your existence is part of that rhythm. Once the changes begin to take place, you must surrender to them. You can't hold on to the old version of your life. It's time to accept the new beginning. And there's power in that. Real transformation can't happen until you surrender to what's already becoming part of your purpose on earth.

Another example is when you realise that your current circle of people no longer fit into your growth. As you build power, you'll be required to connect with people who match your new direction. Your old circle may not want to grow with you. And that's okay. That's part of surrendering to the rhythm of your existence. The more you follow that rhythm instead of fighting it, the more power you'll step into.

No Friendship in Power

In the politics of building power, there are no friends, only enemies or allies.

Some people might not agree with that idea. That's because most people are trained to think from a mindset of mediocrity, especially in the western world. But let me explain it clearly.

First of all, power doesn't attract friends. It attracts opportunists, jealousy, and people who only want to connect because they see something they can gain. Once you gain access to power, everything changes. Even how people look at you, especially if you came from a powerless place.

Friends you once laughed with may now envy you. They may not show it at first, but watch their behaviour. Power can turn friends into foes. And if you study people in high positions, you'll notice they don't really have friends. Even history shows us the same pattern. Powerful people live with a different mindset. And many of them have said this themselves, they live it every day.

The idea of friendship, as most people know it, fits best with a life of comfort and mediocrity. But power is a different lifestyle. It's intentional. It's strategic. It's full of plans and agendas that need to be achieved. That kind of life is not always friendly. It's often lonesome. It's not for everybody. Only a few can handle what comes with power in the long term.

Now, I understand some people may push back on this. They might say, "But I've had the same friends since childhood." Fair enough. So next, let's explore the two levels of success, and how each one affects friendships on your rise to power.

Mediocre Success

When you're at the height of your true power, it will go far beyond what others expected from you. That's what I call high-level success, which I'll go into next. But for now, let's talk about what mediocre success looks like.

Mediocre success is when you reach a goal, which is a good thing, but you haven't hit your full potential. It means you've settled for the lower end of what you're capable of instead of pushing to grow beyond it. This kind of success doesn't shake the room. It's not powerful enough to inspire people to change. It keeps you stuck, playing life safe, with no risk and no real growth.

Because of how low-impact mediocre success is, it's easy to keep the same friends around you. They'll cheer you on, not because your success is inspiring, but because it doesn't make them uncomfortable. It doesn't push them to level up or evaluate their own lives.

So here's the real question, how much have you actually grown over the years? What kind of impact has your success had on the people around you? And if it has had an impact, how powerful has it really been?

High-Level Success

High-level success is the complete opposite of mediocre success. Since we're talking about building power, this type of success goes way beyond what society expects from you. It's about breaking through limits and refusing to be boxed in.

When you start reaching this level, your so-called friends and surroundings will be forced to question themselves. This is where the relationship dynamics shift. And if your success is tied to power-building, your influence will grow even more, and that's when things start to change.

High-level success makes people uncomfortable. It demands more from you and everyone around you. If your friends can't keep up, one of two things will happen, you'll fall out with them, or you'll have to leave them behind.

Power doesn't tolerate mediocrity. It will demand more of you and expose the people who can't rise with you. And if they can't handle the pressure that comes with your elevation, be ready to lose them. All of them. No matter how close they once were.

Now that I've broken down the difference between mediocre and high-level success, I hope it clears things up, especially for those who believe they can keep all their friends while building power. This is the truth behind why there is no friendship in power. The sooner you accept this, the stronger you'll be for the journey ahead.

Be Willing to Let Go of the Old Version of Yourself

Building power will require you to let go of the old version of yourself so you can grow into who you're meant to be. If you keep holding on to the old you, you'll only slow down your progress and hold back the power that's trying to rise within you.

You need to embrace the new version of yourself that's starting to show. Power is about constant evolution. There's no limit to how far you can grow, your goals, your mindset, your vision, your purpose, these things should keep expanding.

The old you has to die so the new you can rise. It's time to step into your new self and own it. No regrets. No hesitation. Take action and take full control of your life. That's how you build true power.

Initiation of Power

Before you begin your pursuit of building power, you must first go through the initiation phase. Without going through this phase, you could put yourself at serious risk, and cause permanent damage that may not be easy to fix, or even possible to repair.

Some people may ask, "What does it mean to be initiated into power?" Let's take a deeper look into what the initiation of power really means.

#1 - Preparation of Power

The first step of the initiation stage is preparing for your position. Keep in mind that even though this is the preparation stage, it can't prepare you for everything that will happen, because power is unpredictable. You never know what's around the corner.

In this stage, you'll begin preparing your mindset to evolve into a higher level of thinking by diving into revolutionary education. You'll also start building up your resilience. This is a tool you'll need to handle the hardships that come with building power.

Resilience is the strength that will carry you through the many battles you'll face. It's also what will help you get through the lonely seasons, especially if you're not used to walking the road alone for long periods of time.

Without going through this preparation stage, you won't succeed in the initiation of power. That's why it's crucial to take part in this phase. It lays the foundation for the journey ahead.

#2 - Understanding the Sacrifices It Takes to Build Power

To succeed in the initiation of power, you must understand the level of sacrifice required to build your power structure. This part of the process is essential. Without it, the average person, especially someone who's never walked this road, may go in blind, not knowing what's truly required.

To build power, you might have to sacrifice the comfort of playing it safe. You might have to let go of certain friendships. And you must be willing to give up the mediocre lifestyle you're used to, in exchange for the path of power.

This path comes with its highs and lows, and you need to accept that. Only then can you truly begin the journey of becoming powerful.

#3 - Understanding the Purpose of Your Power

It's vital to understand the purpose of your power. When you know the reason behind your power, you can use it in a controlled and intentional way.

Without this understanding, you're more likely to misuse your power, which can hurt others, and even destroy you in the process. That's why it's so important to know exactly what your power is for, so you can use it to build, not to damage.

Power used without purpose is dangerous. But when used with clear understanding, it becomes a powerful tool for change.

#4 - Understand Your Role in Your Pursuit of Power

Knowing your role in your journey to power is just as important. When you understand your role, you can carry out your mission with clarity and confidence.

Your role gives you direction. It tells you what your responsibilities are and what kind of power you're supposed to be operating in. Without knowing your role, you'll struggle to stay on course, and your pursuit of power may fall apart before it even begins.

The key takeaway here is this: understand your role so you can get the most out of your journey and fully step into the power that's meant for you.

Chapter 15

—-

Kill The Lies

Building power is a revolutionary act because it brings about real change. In order to build power, you must be willing to accept reality for what it is and let go of any fantasy about life that society has placed on you. Holding onto these illusions will only slow down your progress. Power has no interest in fantasy. It only deals with reality. That's because building power is a real-life experience with real-life consequences. It takes solid, practical strategies to help you take your life to the next level.

If you ever find yourself struggling to accept reality or to let go of fantasy during your journey to power, ask yourself these questions:

- What is it about reality that I find hard to accept?
- What fantasy about life have I been holding onto, and why is it hard to let go?
- Am I afraid of what might happen to me if I fully accept reality?
- What is standing in the way of me seeing life for what it really is?

These questions will help you move forward and ground yourself in truth, which is the foundation of true power.

Reflection

Reflection is an important part of building power because it helps you look at your life through the lens of reality. By doing this, you can observe your current lifestyle and make the changes you feel are needed.

Reflection gives you the chance to reassess your strategy so you can build the kind of power that brings real results. As you go through the power-building journey, you might find that you need to change direction. But even if the route changes, the destination stays the same. You may need to shift how you do things or change the way you think.

When you reflect, think about the following:

#1 - Look at What You Can Do Better

During your reflection period, it's important to look at what you can do better to improve your life to a higher standard. Reflect on how you approach strategies for building power. Engaging in this type of reflection helps you find more efficient ways to get things done, so you can see better results on your power-building journey.

#2 - Discover New Ways of Building Power

Reflection is a great time to discover new ways to build power. There's no single way to get it done. On your journey, you'll face changing circumstances, and these shifts will require you to reflect and adjust. If you've been too rigid in your approach, now is the time to reflect and explore new ways to move forward and diversify your strategy.

#3 - Learn from Your Mistakes

You will make mistakes on the journey to building power, and that's normal. It's part of the process. During this reflection period, it's the best time to look back at your mistakes and make it your mission to learn from them so you don't repeat them. This kind of reflection helps you grow and move forward. Mistakes carry lessons that can bring real wisdom, if you take time to learn.

#4 - Reflect on How You Can Improve

There is always room for improvement on your path to power. Never limit how far you can grow. The moment you stop improving is when you start becoming stagnant. Power demands constant growth. The more you improve, the more power you gain, and the more power you have, the more influence you carry.

The power in reflection is that it holds a mirror directly to your face, allowing you to take an honest look at yourself and the life you're currently living. It gives you the chance to question your own intentions, are they genuine or not? You also get to check whether your integrity is intact, or if you need to make some adjustments in the direction you're going on your journey to build power.

Kill the Lies in Order to Build Power

Building power will require you to destroy the lies that have been fed to you over time. You must be willing to accept reality and people for who they truly are.

Understand this: fantasy and reality don't mix. If you try to blend the two, you'll only confuse yourself and sabotage your rise to power. On this journey, you'll come face to face with the harsh truth of what power really looks and feels like, and it won't match the illusion you may have had in your mind.

You have to kill the illusions you once believed were real and replace them with hard truth. Lies will keep you in a slave-like state of being. Lies manipulate, control, and ultimately destroy your power. That's why it's vital to kill every single lie before it blinds you from the real world that lies ahead.

Don't be afraid to let go of the illusion. Reality isn't as bad as it may seem, once you accept it and are ready to live with it. Killing the lies you've been told is one of the best things you can do for your journey. It will sharpen your focus and strengthen your power-building experience in the long run.

Be OK with Being Underestimated

In today's emotionally triggered society, some people take it personally when they're underestimated. They see it as an insult to their identity, often because they lack emotional intelligence. But what many don't realise is this: being underestimated actually gives you an advantage.

When people don't expect much from you, they're not watching you. That gives you the freedom to work quietly and at your own pace, without pressure. You can make mistakes, learn from them, and build your strength without anyone paying attention. During this time, you have the space to grow your power to a level that becomes hard to break.

When your enemies underestimate you, they won't see you coming. That puts you in a strong position to strike when the time is right. On the flip side, when people expect too much from you, it can make you a target. People start watching your every move, hoping you'll slip up. Some may even go as far as trying to sabotage your progress or take your position of power for themselves.

But when you're underestimated, nobody sees you as a threat. That means fewer attacks, fewer distractions, and more time to plan and plot behind the scenes without pressure or interference.

The lesson here is simple: when building power, don't take it as an insult if people underestimate you. Instead, use that period of underestimation as a strategy. Move in silence. Build in private. And prepare your next move without the weight of eyes watching your every step.

Chapter 16

―――――

Get Hands Dirty

One of the key tools you need for building power is to create a unified narrative that gains the support of the people. It is not enough to throw a message out into society and expect people to support it just because you believe it is worth backing. That is not how it works in the real world.

The narrative you share must be something people can relate to. It needs to speak to their real-life struggles and touch their hearts. If your message does not connect with them in a meaningful way, they will not support it, no matter how strongly you believe in it.

The goal is to get as many people as possible to stand behind your narrative and believe in what you are building. Let's look at a few simple strategies you can use to gain support for a unified narrative.

#1 - Create a Narrative That Is Relatable to the People

Creating a narrative that the people can relate to will be one of the most powerful tools in your journey to build power. A narrative that doesn't connect with others is just a personal belief, it stays with you alone, and that defeats the whole purpose of building a unified message.

Your goal here is to create something that speaks directly to the people's experiences and gets as many of them as possible to stand behind it. How you achieve this will depend on the mood of the people and other factors that might influence how your message is received.

#2 - A Clear Message to Support the Narrative

The message behind your narrative must be clear, straight to the point, and easy to understand. The clearer your message, the easier it will be for people to know what you stand for. Clarity removes confusion and helps people decide if they want to support your mission or not.

#3 - A Narrative That Can Evoke the Emotions of the People

To really make your narrative connect, it may need to touch people emotionally. When you stir emotions, you create a deeper connection, and people are more likely to support what you are saying. But be careful, this isn't about manipulating feelings. If people sense you're playing with their emotions just to gain support, it will backfire and they may turn against you. That can damage everything you've built.

#4 - Identify the Type of Message You Want to Convey Within the Unified Narrative

When you present your narrative, make sure you know exactly what kind of message you are trying to deliver. You want your message to be specific, sharp, and powerful so it leaves a strong impression. If the people can clearly understand and feel the weight of your message, they are more likely to rally behind it.

Be Willing to Get Your Hands Dirty

Building power is a lifestyle that requires you to get your hands dirty. That doesn't mean causing chaos or doing anything reckless. It means being willing to face everything that comes with this life once you commit to it.

You'll need to accept that the game of power is not clean. It's messy. There will be many opposers who are more than happy to play dirty. You have to be ready to deal with it. On your rise to power, you'll carry a lot of dirt on your shoulders. Most of that dirt won't be yours, it will be what others throw at you. That can include betrayal, disrespect, manipulation, character attacks, and more.

That's why I say you need to be willing to get your hands dirty. It's part of the game. Not everyone is built for it, especially in today's world where many people are too fragile to handle the pressure. To survive and thrive in this journey, you need a heart of steel. Anything softer won't last.

Not Everyone Deserves Your Mercy

As you rise in power, people will try to sabotage your mission in ways you never expected. The betrayal will be painful. Unfortunately, that's part of the journey. You can't avoid it, you just have to accept it.

But here's what you need to understand: not everyone deserves your mercy. The people who keep trying to derail you don't deserve your kindness, especially if your mission is for the good of others. We don't live in a fair world where doing the right thing always gets rewarded.

In the power game, some of your enemies will go after you with no mercy. They'll do whatever it takes to destroy what you're building. And if you try to play noble and show mercy to the wrong people, it will cost you. It could even destroy everything you've worked for.

This might sound cold to someone who's never walked this path, but it's reality. When you step into the world of power, you must be prepared to protect yourself and your mission at all costs. Keep that in mind as you move forward.

Don't Operate Below Your Potential

On your journey to power, you need to understand that rising up means never operating below your potential. If anything, you should be pushing to operate above it. Operating below your potential is doing yourself a disservice, and it will only slow down or block your power-building process.

If there is anything or anyone in your life that is limiting your rise, it's your responsibility to remove those things or people, no hesitation. You are not here to shrink yourself to make others feel more comfortable. It's not your job to babysit people's insecurities or manage their feelings about your growth.

The philosophy of building power encourages you to rise to the highest level of your potential, unapologetically. When you hold yourself back, you risk living in frustration and resentment. You begin to resent your life, yourself, and even others, not because of what they've done, but because you know deep down that you could've done better. You know you didn't push yourself as far as you could have.

Society will try to box you in. It will feed you a script; go to school, go to college, get a job, and all the while, those in power are controlling the world while you settle into a powerless routine, never knowing what you're really capable of.

The truth is simple. The philosophy of building power doesn't accept playing small. You must break free from this powerless cycle. Do whatever it takes to rise to your full potential. Not half. Not some. But all of it. By any means necessary.

Break Free of the Illusion of Happiness

To build power, you need to break free of the illusion of happiness. Building power has nothing to do with being happy. Some people may disagree with this, and I understand why, because society is fixated on the false idea of happiness.

Ask yourself this: do we experience happiness every single day? The obvious answer is no. We only feel happiness in moments, and those moments come and go. So if happiness is temporary, why do we spend so much time chasing a feeling that never stays? Wouldn't it be better to just accept life as it is, with all its ups and downs?

To build power, you must find peace in the decisions you make to move forward in life. These decisions aren't about you being happy, and they're not about making others happy either. It's about doing what's best for the mission of taking your power to the next level.

The illusion of happiness and the process of building power do not go together. If you try to chase both, you won't rise. You'll keep getting held back by the need to feel good instead of doing what actually needs to be done. The truth is, most of your decisions on this journey won't feel good. They'll be necessary for your growth. That's why the sooner you break free of the illusion of happiness, the easier it will be to build real power.

Power only deals with what's real. Illusion deals with what's fake. And illusion is the enemy of power.

Some may ask, how do you gain power from letting go of the illusion of happiness? You gain power by freeing yourself from chasing a feeling that was never meant to last. You start to realise that you're not responsible for anyone else's happiness. That understanding gives you a sense of freedom. You're no longer carrying the weight of a lie. And that gives you the strength to accept life on your terms. That is where your real power begins.

Get Rid of the Illusion of People Being Happy for You

In the philosophy of power, you must get rid of the illusion that people will be happy for you as you rise. On your journey to power, depending on how far you go, many people will not be happy for your success, even if they smile in your face and say they are.

I understand it can be disappointing when you find out that your so-called closest friends are not genuinely happy for you during your rise to power. You may have thought they would be happy for you every step of the way. That might sound good in theory, but in reality, it is not always the case.

To truly build power, you must find happiness within yourself and not depend on outside sources. When you get rid of the illusion of external happiness, you stop seeking validation from others and begin to own your power.

Expecting people to be happy for you can lead to you giving your power away instead of holding onto it. Let go of the expectation. Be happy for yourself. That is where real power begins.

Chapter 17

Stay Detached Always

On your rise to power, it is wise not to have any expectations from anybody. In today's world, which some may call modern-day Babylon, we have to admit that many people in western society are struggling when it comes to principles, morals, self-respect, and how they treat one another.

In a society like this, it's not smart to build expectations of people, because it will often lead to disappointment. The only thing you should expect from people is the character they show you, and nothing more.

When building power, people you try to work with might not always meet your expectations. So the best thing you can do is to set expectations for yourself instead. When you expect too much from others, you're giving away your power. You're putting your energy into people who may not be able to meet your standards, and that can take a toll on you.

But when you expect nothing from anyone, you stay in control. You keep your focus on building power without carrying the burden of being let down. Let go of expectations. Keep your energy and power for yourself.

Don't Attach Yourself to Anybody or Anything

When building power, one of the best things you can practice is not attaching yourself to anybody or anything. The dynamics of power are constantly evolving and changing.

Different people will come and go on your journey, so it would not be wise to get too attached to anyone during this process.

The more you remain detached, the more power and control you will have. This doesn't mean having power over people. It means having more control over yourself and your own life.

For example, on your power-building journey, people will enter and exit your life due to the changes that come with growth. What you need to understand is that everyone has an expiry date in your life. Some will stay longer than others. And if you want to move forward in power, you will have to let a lot of people go.

Sometimes, it will hurt to release certain people, especially those you never thought you'd part ways with. But this is part of the process. I advise you not to take this personally. I understand that this may be easier said than done because we are human, but if you take it too personally, it will harm your power-building journey. It will weaken you both emotionally and mentally.

This is why it's important to follow what I call the detachment philosophy. It means understanding why you must stay emotionally detached while building power. This doesn't mean you should become cold or lack compassion. It simply means that staying detached is a survival strategy for power.

Think about it. If you allowed yourself to be consumed by every emotion you feel on the way to power, you would fall apart before you ever truly experience the life of power, including all its highs and lows.

The wisdom I want you to take from this is simple. If you allow yourself to get too attached to people while pursuing power, you will become a victim of those attachments. That can become a major reason for your downfall. Getting emotionally attached in the world of power makes you vulnerable, and vulnerable people are the easiest to break.

Play Your Position

One key part of building power is learning to play your position. This position of power is one you create for yourself. I like to call it a self-made position, because it's not given to you or dictated by anyone else. You choose it. You align yourself with it.

To play your position means knowing your strengths, your skills, and your abilities. But more than that, it's about using them. These tools are what you need to push yourself to the next level. Your position is not just about where you stand, it's about how you move. And if you know how to move in your lane, you will gain the influence and results that come with power.

Replace Babylonian celebrations with your own agendas and plan your next power moves

To build power in modern day Babylon you will need to set your own agendas of power and plan each of your power moves in order to increase your influence over the people. So first of all, let us acknowledge the common celebrations of the West that many of us engage in each year, and then we can delve into how we can replace them with agendas and planning power moves.

#1 - Christmas and Easter

One of the common things about Easter and Christmas is that both of these holidays give a two-week break for people working in the education sector. The philosophy of building power in this case offers you an option. Instead of using this time for celebration, use it to create an agenda that will increase your influence and power This is the perfect time to plan your next power moves for both the short and long term.

The philosophy of building power that I share with you does not encourage you to take part in mediocre Babylonian celebrations that keep you distracted. These holidays also quietly push you to spend money on things that don't bring any return. Your money ends up going right back into the system, which leaves you with nothing. The same system that takes your money is the one that keeps you disempowered.

The philosophy of building power does not allow you to remain in a powerless position. To empower yourself during these holiday periods, it is strongly advised to step away from both celebrations and instead invest your time and money into your own power. Don't give your financial strength to something that gives you nothing in return.

#2 - Valentine's Day

Again, Valentine's Day is another distracting holiday that encourages people to spend money on the illusion of two people trying to show how much they love each other. For those who celebrate Valentine's Day, this message may come across as offensive, but the philosophy of building power is not here to comfort your feelings or soften the truth. It is not responsible for how you choose to interpret the message.

What this philosophy does offer is an alternative to how you can approach Valentine's Day.

Instead of focusing on the so-called love you claim to have for someone else, why not use this day to invest some of that love into yourself? The real question is, how much do you actually love yourself? When was the last time you truly took care of yourself?

The point I want to make here is that there is real power in self-love. The more love you give to yourself, the more power you gain. That power builds your self-worth and self-esteem, and it gives you the confidence and strength you need for the journey of building power.

Calculated Warfare

During the process of building power, it is highly advisable that you engage in calculated warfare as a strategy to reach your goal. In the battlefield of building power, every move you make has to be well thought out and planned. The philosophy of power does not encourage random or careless actions that can mess up your journey.

The whole point of calculated warfare is to be organised and intentional with every step you take. Let us look into a few strategies that might help you in the battlefield of building power.

#1 - False Sense of Predictability

A good strategy to use while rising to power is creating a false sense of predictability among the people. Some may ask, why use this strategy? Let me explain.

When people believe they know your every move, they get comfortable. They drop their guard. Their alertness is low because, in their mind, you are no threat. You appear to be doing the same thing every day, and that makes them feel safe around you. But behind the scenes, you are making strategic moves no one sees.

To use this strategy properly, you must stay disciplined and avoid the urge to prove anything to anyone. If people assume you are predictable, let them. Do not waste your time trying to show them otherwise.

This approach keeps you off the radar and gives you time to quietly build your power. Then, when the time is right, you strike. Remember, this strategy is only temporary. As your power grows, people will eventually notice. By the time they do, you should have built enough protection around yourself to defend against any enemies that try to sabotage you on the battlefield of power.

#2 - Don't Show All Your Power in One Hand

In the battlefield of power, there are things you must understand, and one of those things is to never show all your power in one hand. Think about this carefully. If you show people all the power you have, you make yourself a target. You will attract jealousy and envy, even if you don't mean to.

It's up to you to equip yourself with the knowledge and understanding of how people think, feel, and behave around someone with power. If you don't do this properly, it could delay your rise. Instead of rising smoothly, you'll spend too much time defending yourself from unnecessary attacks. That pressure can lead to burnout, and that burnout could eventually bring you to your knees at the mercy of those trying to sabotage you.

So it's important to hold some of your power back until the right time. Don't show everything. Stay calm and move with steady purpose.

#3 - Do Not Expose Your Agenda of Power

As you rise to power, never reveal your full agenda to the public. This kind of information is not for everyone. It doesn't mean you can't trust anyone, but you never know when someone might change their mind about you or your mission.

When someone changes their heart about a situation, it can lead to betrayal. This happens often in the power game, which is why you keep your agenda to yourself. If you expose it too early, you leave yourself wide open for attacks. The goal here is to carry out your agenda, not announce it. Let your moves speak louder than your plans.

#4 - Blend In with the Masses

Blending in with the masses is a wise strategy to use when building power. We are often told that standing out as an individual makes you unique, which is true to some extent. But in the battlefield of power, standing out too much makes you an easy target. It means you're easily recognisable, and people can spot you from a distance.

The whole point of blending in is to avoid bringing too much attention to yourself. You want to move through your rise to power with as little pressure as possible. The less pressure you face, the more effectively you can move around and make your next power moves without being blocked or attacked along the way.

Secret Enemies Within Your Circle

On your rise to power, you will have secret enemies around you. Most people are not aware of this, which is why I'm pointing it out now, so you are not shocked when it happens. This is part of understanding the reality of how power works.

As you start to gain more influence, you'll naturally attract enemies. But your most dangerous enemies are not usually the ones outside your circle. They are more likely to be the ones within it. Some people might ask, "Why would someone in my circle become an enemy?"

Let me explain. The people outside your circle don't really know you. They don't have access to personal details or inside information that could be used against you. Without information, there's very little they can do to hurt or sabotage you.

But the people inside your circle do know you. They know your strengths, weaknesses, plans, and patterns. That's what makes them far more dangerous.

Now, the people within your circle who have personal information about you are definitely more of a threat than outsiders. This is because they know so much about you that can be used as a tool to bring you down on your journey to building power. What makes it worse is if those people are jealous or envious of your position. Some of them may even fantasise about taking your place. They just haven't acted on those thoughts yet.

But if they ever see an opportunity to take your position, they might try it. These are the people I'm referring to as your secret enemies. They smile in your face, congratulate you on your success, and know how to hide their jealousy and envy so well that you may not even notice it. Sometimes, they'll throw little underhanded jokes about your achievements and play them off like harmless banter. But deep down, there's a dark resentment growing inside them, something they've been hiding for a long time. One day, they won't be able to hide it anymore, and it will start to show in their words and actions toward you.

This kind of behaviour usually becomes clear the more your power and influence grow. The lesson here is this: in the battlefield of power, it's not the people outside your structure you need to worry about most. It's the ones inside your structure that you must keep your eyes on. These are the people who know your business, and if they ever have a change of heart, they could betray you and even leak information to outsiders. That creates cracks in your power structure that can be used to bring you down.

It's your job to keep an eye on those around you, no matter how close they seem. If you notice any strange or suspicious behaviour from them, don't ignore it. Investigate it and get to the bottom of it.

Chapter 18

Soldiers Not Followers

In a new world where social media dominates everyday life for most people, and where followers and subscribers are the new normal, it's important to understand something. Just because influencers online have a lot of followers or high subscriber counts, it doesn't necessarily mean they are important people. It just means they've managed to put out content that people enjoy, and because of that, people choose to follow them.

In the dynamics of building power, having followers and subscribers doesn't mean much. The reason is simple, online followers are just that, followers. They're not always taking real action to bring about any kind of change. Most are just sitting back and letting themselves be entertained by whatever new content pops up.

The philosophy of power says that it's not enough to just have followers. What you really need are soldiers. People who are ready to be active participants in helping you build power and grow your influence among the people so the real work can get done.

Pretend to be dumb to outsmart your competitors, enemies, and foes

Some people may not agree with the idea of pretending to be dumb to outsmart your opposition on your rise to power. But what they don't understand is that this can be a very smart strategy. When your opposition sees that you're highly intelligent, you may be viewed as a threat. Once that happens, they'll likely create more obstacles for you. You don't need to deal with more obstacles than necessary, especially in the early stages of your journey to power.

Once you're seen as the "dummy" of the group, your opposition will begin to underestimate you. They'll think they have the upper hand and believe you're not capable of making major power moves. This gives you the advantage of moving under the radar, plotting and calculating your next move without any distractions.

Remember, in the battlefield of power, there's no need to prove you're the smartest. The smarter you appear, the more of an open target you become. As long as you know how smart you are, there's no reason to prove anything to others. Pretending to be dumb is a tool you can use to get ahead. It allows you to trick your enemies into thinking you're not a threat, buying you the time you need to plan and act.

However, be careful. Not everyone will fall for this trick. There's always someone in the background watching closely. Never underestimate your opposition's ability to figure you out. The goal is that by the time they catch on, you've already made your move, and it's too late for them to stop you.

Know which battles to fight

On your pursuit to power, you must understand that not every battle should be fought. Not every situation needs your attention. Think about it. If you tried to fight every battle that came your way, you'd eventually burn out. In the battlefield of power, it's wise to save your energy and focus only on battles that are worth your time.

Before you step into any battle, take a moment to study it. Ask yourself, is it worth fighting? The philosophy of building power includes knowing when to surrender. Surrendering isn't a sign of weakness. It's simply acknowledging the truth of what you're facing. Some battles are not meant to be fought, and that's okay.

The key lesson here is to be strategic about which battles you take on. Jumping into every fight without thinking is a form of power suicide. It means you're wasting energy and giving away your power for no good reason.

Understand the nature of loyalty

In the world of power, you have to understand how loyalty works. In everyday life, when someone stops being loyal, people often feel heartbroken, disappointed, or even angry. But these strong emotions usually come from not fully understanding how loyalty operates between people.

In the dynamics of power, loyalty is often based on what someone can gain from you at the time. When something better comes along, people won't hesitate to switch sides. If what you offer is no longer useful to them, they'll move on.

Loyalty is rarely about deep personal connection. It's about benefit. That's the truth. So when someone you trusted changes sides, don't take it personally. It's not always about you. It's just how power works.

Your job is to understand this nature of loyalty and accept it for what it is. Once you do, you'll stop letting people's shifting loyalties shake you emotionally. Instead, you'll keep moving forward on your journey to power with focus and clarity.

Do not allow yourself to be bought

In the dynamics of power, you must understand one thing clearly. Never allow yourself to be bought. If you let yourself be bought, you lose your power. The person who buys you is the one who gets to decide your worth, and that leaves you powerless.

When you look at celebrities and their lifestyles, some of you might think, "I wish I could live like that." But what you don't know is that many of these celebrities are just rich slaves. They've allowed themselves to be bought. They can't speak freely on certain topics or speak out against injustice, because if they do, they risk losing their sponsors, endorsements, or even their whole careers.

Some are even placed on the Forbes list, where the world is told what their net worth is without any input from them. That alone tells you who really holds the power, Forbes or the celebrity? The truth is, most of them don't have real control over their own lives. They're still slaves, controlled by the very industry that pays them.

The philosophy of power does not support the idea of being bought. It does not empower you in any way. If anything, being bought keeps you stuck in a state of submission. Whoever can buy you will control how you see yourself, how others see you, and even the story the world tells about you.

Don't allow your pain to consume you, make it your lethal weapon

On your way to building power, you will likely go through pain. You may lose people you were once close with. You might fall out with family. You'll face hard situations that hurt.

But here's the truth. You cannot let that pain consume you. If you let it take over, it will cloud your judgment. Worse, it can block your ability to build power. But if you flip the script and turn your pain into a lethal weapon, that pain can make you unstoppable.

Let your pain be the fuel that drives you. Let it make you stronger. Let it teach you wisdom. Use it as a lesson and a shield. If a mistake led to your pain, let that pain protect you from making the same mistake again.

There is power in learning how to control and master your emotions, especially your pain. If you can hold that power without letting it break you, you'll become sharper, stronger, and more fearless than you've ever been. Pain, when handled the right way, can be one of your deadliest weapons on the battlefield of power.

Chapter 19

——

Hunter Not Prey

In the dynamics of power, you must always make sure you are the hunter and not the prey. To be the hunter means to always stay hungry on your rise to power. That means knowing what your agenda is, staying in a freethinking state of mind, and not allowing yourself to be easily influenced by others. Get rid of any naivety about how the world of power really works. Accept human nature for what it is, not what you want it to be. Keep your mind sharp by feeding it new knowledge so you can grow and evolve into a better version of yourself.

By doing all these things, you'll be able to keep yourself in a hunter's position and avoid becoming the prey.

In today's modern society, a lot of average people live in the prey position. They are easily manipulated. Many carry a victim mindset. Whether they do it on purpose or not, they make themselves easy targets for others to feed on.

You see it all the time on social media. People post videos of themselves crying, showing their vulnerabilities, or even exposing how ignorant they are. This opens the door for manipulators to spot your weaknesses and use them against you. Their aim is to keep you powerless while they continue to rise.

Play the role of a servant, secretly think like a ruler

In the battlefield of power, one of the most effective strategies you can use to get ahead is to play the role of a servant while secretly thinking like a ruler. When you play the role of a servant, you are not seen as a threat. Your opposition may let their guard down, thinking that you will never strike because of your consistent role play as someone who simply serves.

What your opposition does not know is that you are quietly plotting to rule and take over. They cannot see your plan because they do not see the ruler within you. All they see is the role you play as a loyal servant.

This is not an easy task to pull off. It takes a special kind of character and discipline to succeed with this strategy. Let us look into a few tools that can help you carry out this goal effectively.

#1 - Discipline

To maintain your role as a servant, you must stay disciplined. At times, you might feel frustration boiling inside you. This can happen because of the strong king-like mindset you carry, and because of that, you may feel tempted to step out of line and show your opposition what you are really made of. But in this case, I highly advise you to hold back. If you react too soon, you will only make yourself a target and alert your opposition to watch you more closely.

#2 - Smile

A smart strategy to add to your servant role is simply to smile, even when you do not feel like it. When you smile in front of your opposition, it makes you look pleasant and approachable. Nobody fears someone who smiles and seems friendly. What they do not realise is that your smile is hiding your real intentions, making your true thoughts completely undetectable. This gives you a powerful advantage, because now you can strike without warning. Nothing is more dangerous than a quiet attack hiding in plain sight.

#3 - Be consistent in your servant role

To succeed in your servant role, you must stay consistent. Keep in mind, the time you play this role will depend on your situation. There is no set date when you stop acting as the servant. But for as long as you are playing the role, you must not break character. You do not want to give off any strange signals that might alert your opposition. Stay in position until you are strong and stable enough to shift your power to the next level.

#4 - Appear to be harmless

As you continue to play the role of the servant, another powerful strategy is to appear harmless. Think about it in your own life. Look at the people you consider harmless. These are usually people you think would not hurt a fly. You feel relaxed around them, with your guard completely down. That same feeling is what you want your opposition to feel. In the power game, this works well because you are not seen as a threat. Your harmless look has them fooled, and now they are relaxed. At this point, they become an open target.

You now have the upper hand and many ways you can strike, giving you a huge advantage.

Operate like a secret agent

In the dynamics of building power, there is a certain way you need to move to increase your chances of success, and that is to operate like a secret agent. To gain power over your opposition, you need to be somewhat of a spy. You have to actively play the role of a spy on your competitors, which means saying less and observing more. When I say play the role of a spy, I mean paying close attention to how power really works.

For example, let's say you are in a boardroom meeting with some of the most powerful elites. Your goal is to learn about them by studying the language of power they use to express themselves. Study how they think, how they move, and how they execute their goals. Only speak when it is appropriate, because the less you speak, the more you can learn. Your mission is to gather as much information as you can to get ahead in the dynamics of power.

You must never reveal too much about yourself. This is not the time to share your plans or future intentions. Always remember, your role is to remain the secret agent, not just in the example of sitting in a boardroom, but also in your everyday life as you rise in power.

The power you gain from acting like a secret agent is the ability to gather valuable information without limits. The person with the most information can use it as leverage to advance in the game of power. This is no different from how the elites rule over the masses. They have access to knowledge that most people do not, which is why the majority are ruled by the powerful few.

Build a wise counsel with like-minded people

On your journey to building power, it is highly advisable to form an alliance with like-minded people to create what I like to call a wise counsel. This circle, including yourself, will be made up of people who have gained wisdom through experience. It will be a group filled with knowledge, where you can share and advise one another on how to solve problems and make sound decisions that lead to real results in your power-building journey.

The main goal of this wise counsel is to help you stay balanced by surrounding yourself with people who share similar ideals. This group can also serve as a tool to influence the wider public in a powerful and strategic way.

One thing you must understand is that not everyone should be invited into this circle. Not everyone has the same intentions. Some may come in and bring confusion or even corruption because they don't understand or respect what the wise counsel stands for. This is not something you promote like an open event for the world to see.

To build this circle, you need to speak to different people and watch closely to see if they have the right qualities to be part of your wise counsel. For those who have never formed a circle like this before, let's look at how that can be done.

#1 - Go out with the intention of meeting people

When it comes to meeting people, there is no specific place where it must happen, so don't expect to meet potential members of your wise counsel in one set location. You could meet them anywhere, even at local events near you. If you're someone who doesn't go out much, now is the time to start. You won't meet anyone by isolating yourself from society. Always remember that your main reason for going out to these events is to network and meet people you can potentially build with.

#2 - Study the person you are talking to

When you're out meeting people, don't just talk for the sake of it. Make sure you're communicating with purpose. The aim is to study the character of the person you're talking to without judging them. Your mission is to gather as much information about them as you can. Ask meaningful questions and make sure your level of questioning is intentional.

#3 - Seek out whether they have the qualities to be a part of the wise counsel

As you talk to new people, keep in mind that you are looking to see if they have the qualities to be part of the wise counsel you want to build. The qualities you may want to look out for include knowledge, wisdom, and a deep understanding of humanity. For this task, you'll need to use your discernment. Discernment is a life skill that comes with experience and engaging with different types of people. Make sure your discernment skills are sharp and ready so you can complete this task effectively.

#4 - Schedule a time to meet up with the potential members of the wise counsel

After you've gone through the stage of figuring out whether the people you spoke to, whether at a local event or any other kind of social gathering, have the qualities to be potential members of the wise counsel, the obvious next step is to exchange contact details. Once that's done, schedule a time to meet up outside of wherever you first met them. Choose a public place where you can spend time together and get to know them better. This allows you to observe their personality and get a real sense of who they are. Think of this meet-up as an icebreaker, something to help build familiarity and lay the foundation for a long-term relationship that can eventually lead to forming a wise counsel.

During this first scheduled meet-up, it's a good idea to talk about how often you'll be meeting moving forward. You could start with something simple like a once-a-month meet-up. Be sure to set agendas for what you want to accomplish during each session. This keeps your time focused and makes sure progress is actually being made each time you meet.

Be the person people need

In order to be a dynamic power force, it is best to put yourself in a position where people need you. When you are someone who is needed, you become high in demand, especially if what you offer is rare. Make yourself a useful resource that benefits both yourself and others. There is real power in being the person people rely on because you become a force to be reckoned with. If you are a resource to yourself and others, you can use that as a way to increase your influence in society.

There are many people in modern-day society who live without any real purpose. If you pay attention to those living without direction, you'll see they have little to no use to anyone, not even themselves. That makes them disposable, because they bring no value to society. At that point, those types of people become powerless due to their lack of usefulness.

It is your responsibility to improve your self-worth. It is your responsibility to add value to yourself so that others can respect you. The philosophy of power does not support living life as a disposable human being. In the dynamics of power, disposable people have no place. That is why I stress the importance of being the person people need.

Don't allow people to use you for free

In the dynamics of power, you must understand that there will be people who want to use you for what they need. Some people may say that if someone is using you, then they are not genuine. But in reality, whether we want to admit it or not, we all get used. We just don't always say it out loud. Being used by someone isn't the issue. The real issue is how it is done. If someone is trying to use you under the illusion of being your friend, then that is foul play, because they are being disingenuous instead of being upfront about their real intentions. As an individual, if you allow someone to use you for free, that is also a mistake on your part. You must never allow anyone to use you for free. It is your duty to let them know that using you comes with a cost. The cost may not always be money, but it will have a price, and it is up to you to decide what that price will be.

Think about it like this. In order to develop yourself on your rise to power, you'll realise that even developing yourself isn't

127

free. The cost of your personal development includes money, time, and effort. So with that being the case, ask yourself this: if you are paying a price for your own growth, then why would you let anyone else use you for free, when you are constantly paying to level up and build your power? This is why many people feel upset when they realise they've been used. They gave away their power for free and got nothing in return.

The power in not allowing yourself to be used for free comes from knowing your worth. You must always remember that your worth comes at a cost. Never let anyone take advantage of that, especially in the dynamics of power where everyone is using someone for something. Being used is not the problem. It's how you allow yourself to be used that's the real issue. The name of the game here is to never give your power away for free, because even your own power came at a cost.

Chapter 20

Know The Rules

When building power you must understand the rules that are being played in the real world. Before you go into the dynamics of power, take the time to study the rules and align yourself with them to get the results you need. One of the rules you must come to terms with when engaging in the rules of power is that nobody cares about your emotions. The dynamics of power include a level of ruthlessness. The small percentage of people that have the power, which I refer to as the elites, play by a different set of rules which includes manipulation. They play by whatever rules get them the results they need, meaning they don't play fair at all.

The people in power will do you dirty to make sure they get their agendas met, regardless of the damage they cause. They are the ones that control the narrative of power and how it operates in society. The average person does not have any control of how the dynamics of power operate on a day-to-day basis. This is why I am saying that if you want to gain any power or influence in this current climate, you will have to align yourself with the current rules of power that are in effect. When the odds are against you, it will be required of you to do what is necessary to flip those odds into your own favour.

For those in society who may not want to play by the current rules of power and think they can bring their influence into the world with love, peace, nobleness, morals, and principles, which all sound great in the ideal sense, understand this. In the dynamics of power that we witness in today's world, you will not get rewarded for being any of those things. Instead, you will get run over and left for dead. As harsh as that sounds, that is the reality we live in. The elite powers of the world have designed humanity to operate in an unethical way just to survive on a daily basis. This is why there is so much corruption running rampant worldwide.

#1 - Manipulation

Manipulation is a tactic that the elites in power use to get their agendas executed. They will manipulate anybody at any cost, even if it leads to tragedy. The mindset the elites have is a by-any-means-necessary type of mentality. So if they see manipulation as a tactic to get the job done, they will use it with no hesitation. Some of you may say that manipulation is unethical, and yes, that may be true. But the people in control of power do not care about that. They are not concerned about morals or principles. All they care about is getting the task done, no matter the cost.

#2 - Greed

Greed is another rule that the elites in power live by. By nature, they are takers and gatekeepers of power and resources. They take and rarely give anything back in return. Even when they already have more than enough money and resources among themselves, they still take the little that the everyday person has to make themselves even more powerful.

#3 - Lies

Another strategy the people in power use is telling lies to brainwash society and keep people in a subservient state. For example, politicians make false promises that they will bring change, but as soon as they get into office, they fail to deliver on those promises. That's because they never really intended to change anything. The politician already had their own agenda. They know that lies bring comfort to society, and they use that to their own advantage.

Another lie pushed by the elites in power is the idea that if you go to school, go to college, and get a job, you will be successful. This is far from the truth. While most people follow this path, the elites have access to information and opportunities that the everyday person is not even aware of.

#4 - No morals

In the dynamics of power in today's world, the people in control do not operate with any kind of morals. We live in a society where people who try to live by morals do not get rewarded. Sadly, the system is not designed that way. The elites in power understand this very well. That's why they are at the top and the moral people are at the bottom. This setup is intentional. The elites do not play by the rules of morality. They play by the rules that help them get the job done, even if it means going against all morals.

#5 - No principles

When it comes to power, the elites don't move with any principles. They play dirty with the goal of winning, especially when their power is at risk. Principles mean nothing to them when it's about keeping their position at the top. So whatever personal values or standards you live by will not apply when you are going up against competitors in the world of power.

#6 - No sympathy

Another truth you must accept in the dynamics of power is that your opposition will show you no sympathy. They see pity as weakness. You might feel it's right to care when someone is struggling because we're all human, but in the world of power, that's not how things work. Your competitors are here to conquer and dominate. They are not looking to be kind or show mercy, so don't expect it.

#7 - No empathy

In the dynamics of power, there is no empathy for your feelings or emotions, or for anyone else's. Sociopath-like behaviour often rules in these circles, whether people admit it or not. It's a very cold world to be a part of. This position of power is not for the faint-hearted but for those with a heart of steel. Do not expect people in power to feel what you feel. They are not capable of that kind of empathy.

#8 - Betrayal

Betrayal is another major force and common tactic used in the dynamics of power. Many people would agree that betrayal is unethical, and that's true. But in the world of power, your feelings about betrayal are not considered. Betrayal is part of the game. So don't go into the battlefield of power trying to apply your own personal rules in a space you don't control. Know your role and understand the rules already in place, because if you don't, you will not survive.

Be neither good nor bad

When building power, don't get caught up in the idea of what kind of person you think you should be. Being in a position of power isn't about being good or bad, it's about doing what's necessary based on the situation. Don't stress about being labelled a bad person just because you made a decision someone didn't like. Remember, as someone on the journey to build power, it's not your job to please others. You're not here to play the good guy. The philosophy of building power is not about being good or bad. It's about doing what needs to be done to reach your goal.

It is not your job to make people happy

On your path to power, one of the biggest mistakes you can make is putting your energy into trying to make everyone happy. That's impossible and will only hold you back. It's not your responsibility to carry the burden of making others feel good. Wasting your time on that will drain your energy and weaken your focus. Instead, save that energy and use it to build yourself up and move to the next level.

Do not negotiate your values to be liked

When building power you must understand that in this dynamic it is not about being liked or loved, you are not building power to suit everybody's needs as that is not how the real world works. You have to be stern and firm with the position you choose to play, meaning you must not be willing to negotiate your values to be liked because you will only end up putting yourself on an endless treadmill trying to please everybody. In power your values is not up for negotiation, if people are not happy with what it is you stand for that is not your problem, that is a problem they will need to deal with among themself which has nothing to do with you. If you spend time negotiating your values just to be liked you will only diminish your own power and find yourself constantly bending to the whim of others, the philosophy of building power does not advocate you to negotiate your values at any given time even if it means you being labelled the bad guy, the power to be gained here is that you are not compromising your values which enhances your level of certainty to move forward without having any self-doubts about your intentions. Unfortunately there is so many people that negotiate their own values just so they can be liked by others which in the end only leaves them in a paralysed position of powerlessness.

Update your value

It is important that while you are building power that you always continue to update your value, updating your value puts you in a position of leverage to increase your power and worth. It is not about just getting to the destination of power, you have to maintain your position and to do this you must not become complacent. Complacency is a disease to maintaining power which is why you constantly update your value and worth, not just for your own benefit but also to be of good service to others. The truth is if you are no longer of value to yourself or others your power will diminish and your influence that you worked so hard to build up will deplete, do not make the mistake of getting too comfortable just because you think you made a success of yourself, there is always room for improvement, updating your value helps you to maintain your position of power. Remember in the dynamics of power there is always a new competitor on the rise that is hungry for success and will do whatever it takes to knock you out of your position in order for them to thrive to the next level.

Create opportunities that can benefit others

In maintaining your power, it is safe to say that it's okay to create opportunities that benefit others and not just yourself.

Creating opportunities only for yourself is a selfish act, and living this way can lead to jealousy, envy, and resentment from others, especially if you're in a position to help provide better opportunities for people.

I'm not saying that everyone is entitled to your help in life. What I am saying is that by sharing opportunities with others, you can form strong partnerships, which in turn can grow your alliance with the people. Always remember that there is more power in numbers than in individualism.

I strongly advise you not to gate-keep opportunities from others. Doing that will only trap you in an individualistic mindset. Your personal strength alone can only take you so far, but having power in numbers can carry you much further. The philosophy here is to empower others so they can help themselves.

Protect yourself in a rigged game

The dynamics of power is a very tricky battlefield to be part of. If you don't take the time to study the game of power, it will take you by surprise because of your lack of knowledge about how dirty this game really is. You must protect yourself at all costs, as the game of power is rigged. It's not set up to benefit everyone. It's built to benefit only the few who hold the power and resources to do as they please, while the average person suffers at the hands of the relentless greed of the elite powers that dominate most people.

Because power rules the majority, it affects how everyday society operates. The society we live in today is a direct reflection of the elite powers in control of the narrative people live by. This makes it even harder for you to navigate, because society, whether people are aware of it or not, acts as a covert protective mechanism that creates a barrier to stop you from bringing any real change to the world.

This covert protective mechanism is a strategic weapon created by the government to protect itself against anyone who dares to challenge its control over the people. You must protect your power in various ways, which we will explore below.

#1 - Do not take it personal

On the journey of building power, you may experience a lot of betrayal, hurt, pain, anger, and a mix of other things that come with the territory of power. One thing I want to highlight is that during this experience, it is in your best interest not to take things personal in the dynamics of power. For example, when you face betrayal on your journey to power, try to understand that it's part of the game. Unfortunately, betrayal is a nature that's built into the process of building power. Sometimes that betrayal will come from the people closest to you, which makes the hurt and pain feel even worse.

I understand that we are all human and have emotions, but I must say that if you take it all too personal, it will only weaken you and bring you to your knees. It will stop you from rising or maintaining your position of power. Take the pain, the hurt, the anger, the rage, and the betrayal and use it as a lesson to sharpen your understanding of how power works in the real world today. The strength you gain from not taking things personal is that you get to hold onto that energy and redirect it in a way that benefits your journey to building power.

#2 - Use your understanding of power as a weapon of protection

Understanding power is key to knowing how to protect yourself from the attacks that will come your way. These attacks are not something you can avoid, they are inevitable. Anyone who steps into power without a real understanding of how it works becomes an open target for people to attack at any time. If you are not prepared to deal with the reality of what comes with building power, you could become a permanent casualty who can't recover.

It is your job to study, learn, and apply your knowledge of how people operate in the world of power. Study their behaviour, learn the strategies they use, and observe how people react to those who hold power. Use that knowledge as a shield to protect yourself so that you don't become easy prey for both societal and elite predators.

#3 - Play by their rules, live by your own philosophy

When you are starting from the bottom and trying to rise in power, you have to understand that you don't get to set the rules. Someone above you already controls how the game is played. If you try to rebel too early and go against the system, you could end your own journey before it even starts. The smart thing to do is put your ego to the side and play by the rules of those in power, while quietly living by your own philosophy.

Some people might not agree with this. They might believe they can go out into the world and fully be themselves, even under someone else's system. They may think you are asking them to give up who they are, but that's not the case. I'm simply telling you that if you want your share of power, there are rules already in place. Whether you like them or not, the rules won't change for you. You must do what needs to be done until you have enough power and influence to move with leverage.

Remember, in the battlefield of power, your personal philosophy should be lived, not told. Never expose it to your competitors. The power in this strategy is that they believe you are fully playing by their rules, while you are quietly following your own plan, waiting for the right moment to act. This is how real rulers of power move, and you are no different. If you want results, follow the formula.

#4 - Keep your thoughts silent

In the battlefield of power, your silence is one of your strongest tools, especially when it comes to your thoughts. Never share your thoughts with your competitors, because doing that only exposes you. Once exposed, they can study you and find ways to defeat you.

In this age of social media, people think sharing every thought makes them relevant. They believe staying loud keeps them seen and respected. But the truth is, being too loud makes you an easy target. It allows your competitors to analyse your mind and use your own thoughts against you.

When you keep your thoughts to yourself, you stay unpredictable. That unpredictability is your protection. Stay quiet, move smart, and only speak when it's absolutely necessary. That's how you keep control of your power.

#5 - Maintain a heart of steel

The dynamics of power is not for the faint hearted. You cannot let your emotions get in the way of your decision making, even if those decisions make others uncomfortable. In the battlefield of power, there is no mercy for those with weak hearts. People who can't stand firm in their decisions will often be their own downfall. Even when the choice is for the greater good of building power, their emotions hold them back.

You must understand that the elite powers of the world are extremely heartless. They don't move based on feelings. They operate by what works and what is necessary, no matter the outcome. The truth is, if you want to play the game of power, your heart needs to be strong enough to handle the ups and downs that come with it. A weak heart will only bring your journey to an early end.

#6 - Masking your intentions through a friendly appearance

On your rise to power, you need to be careful about how you move with your intentions. If you don't handle this correctly, it could stop your progress before it even begins.

For example, if you see two people in the battlefield, who would you suspect more? The one with a cold, mean look or the one with a friendly, harmless appearance? Most people judge by appearances, so by instinct, they focus on the one who looks threatening. The friendly face often goes unnoticed.

That is exactly why a friendly appearance can give you the upper hand. It doesn't raise any alarms. People don't expect danger from someone who seems kind or easy going. This allows you to move quietly and build your power without drawing suspicion. Then, when it's time to act, your move will catch everyone by surprise.

Declare war on your own mediocrity

On your journey to building power, one of the first things you must do before starting your mission is to declare war on your own mediocrity. You need to do this before stepping into the battlefield of power, because mediocrity is a way of life for the average person, while power and dominance are forces that demand respect.

To build power, you must stop settling for the standards society tries to place on you and rise to a level of greatness that even goes beyond what you thought possible for yourself. No longer will you listen to the echo of mediocre messages that were forced on you from childhood to adulthood. No longer will you back down from challenges that are meant to help you grow. No longer will you hold on to mediocre people who block your rise to power. No longer will you run from your calling. No longer will you be a coward because of your fear of the unknown. No longer will you be a slave to the expectations of who and what society says you should be.

No longer will you fear the new version of yourself that's waiting to rise up and take control. A version ready to conquer, not by controlling others, but by taking full control of your own life with no limits. No longer will you sabotage your own power just to make others feel comfortable. No longer will you bow to mediocrity. It's time to rise against it. Destroy the fear inside you and declare war on your own mediocrity. Let a new, more powerful version of yourself rise and take shape in the society you live in.

The circulation of power

It is important to understand that in order to maintain your position of power, you must create something I like to call the circulation of power. The circulation of power is a philosophy that requires you not to keep all your power to yourself. It is ok to share your power with others.

The circulation of power, when used correctly, becomes a source of energy from the people that circles its way back to you. Its main purpose is to keep you energised, especially during times when you may feel burnt out from the intensity of the battlefield of power. To maintain this circulation, you will need to empower members of society by sharing valuable information and resources that create opportunities not just for yourself but for others as well.

By doing this, people may want to align themselves with you, which helps you build allies and relationships that support your mission to build power. If you keep all the power to yourself, it can create jealousy, envy, and potentially turn people into enemies. Remember, your mission is to build with the people, not against them. So it is in your best interest to engage in the circulation of power to grow your influence among the people.

But while doing this, move with caution. Do not be blindly naive and think you can share your power with everyone. Believe it or not, there is always someone in the shadows secretly plotting against you. They will smile in your face and stab you in the back when they get the chance. The circulation of power is best used with your wise counsel of trusted people who are like-minded and share your principles and philosophy.

Chapter 21 -

Keep Goals Invisible

In the process of building power, it is important that you keep your goals invisible. I understand that you may want to share your goals with people. Maybe you are excited about your future goals, or maybe you want to share good news with people, thinking that they will be happy for you. In reality, making your goals visible can bring disruption to your progress. Some people could secretly steal your ideas and make them their own goals before you even start working on those goals yourself. Sometimes people will even go to the extent of creating hidden barriers to prevent you from becoming successful, which is why I say to keep your goals invisible.

In the battlefield of power, exposing your goals can make you a target for study, where your competitors can use that information as leverage to know your every move, knowing when and how you strike. These are not the type of moves anybody should know but you.

In the age of social media, where everybody appears to be doing well, or for those that are actually striving and feel the need to show it all off for likes and clout for everybody to see as a form of social proof, let me say this: the more you expose and show off your goals to the visible eye, you are potentially creating secret enemies that will not make themselves known to you, which could be a problem for you in the long term. The worst thing you can have is a bunch of secret enemies plotting your downfall but yet smiling in your face and then striking you when you do not see it coming.

Remember, you have nothing to prove to anyone. If people want to believe that you do not have any goals, let them think it. All the better for you, because now you can make your moves silently and strategically and strike at any time without them knowing.

Transparency Must Be Used with Caution

In the game of power, transparency must be used with caution. Too much transparency can expose your weakness and make you a target for predators and people alike to take advantage of you. When building power, it is not wise to be overly transparent with people, especially in the battlefield. Unfortunately, we live in a predatory world where the strong prey on the weak, naive, and feeble people of society.

There is a time and a place for transparency, which should only be used when necessary. Transparency is not to be used impulsively because people will use your transparency against you if they think it is necessary. Almost every day in the online world, you see people exposing their feelings of sorrow, sadness, pain, anger, and frustration. I understand some people may say that it's very human to see people express their feelings publicly, but in the dynamics of power, this is seen as weakness.

Look at it like this: the same feelings of transparency that you expose can be the same thing that causes your own downfall. Being too transparent means you are giving away too much of your power to people. It is important that you use transparency in its correct capacity. So, for example, if you are trying to build a long-term relationship of trust with someone, then it may be in your best interest to use transparency as a tool to accomplish this task. But even then, the amount of information you share should come with a limit. Never show your full hand of transparency in the battlefield of power, as it may be used as a weapon to destroy you.

Do Not Be Fixed in Character

Building power will require you to shift characters from time to time. In your position of power, you cannot afford to be stuck in a fixed character. You must be willing to change the way you do things. I say this because the position of power is not a fixed role. You will need to use different parts of your character to navigate through the complexities of the different types of experiences that come with playing this unique position. You will need to adapt to different situations at hand, despite how you feel about them.

Let's explore the different characters you will have to play in your position of power:

#1 - The Silent Character

In your position of power, you will at times need to remain silent. Your silence will be used to watch, listen, and observe what is happening around you. This is the time to study the actions of people. This is the time you keep your emotions, intentions, and words in complete silence, as it will be a necessary strategy to use on your rise to power. As we must remind ourselves, silence is a good tool to use to move up in the ranks of power without too much disturbance, due to your silent movements being difficult to detect.

#2 - The Ruthless Character

In your position of power, you will be required to be ruthless at times. Your competitors operate within the same character, so do not think for one second that you being the good Samaritan is going to change this reality. You need to be just as ruthless as they are to accomplish your goals. I am not saying to behave like some sort of tyrant or treat people like mere peasants. What I am saying is that in the dynamics of power, you will not always be able to show pity for others, especially if they betray or violate you in any way that is unacceptable.

At times, you need to be ruthless in your pursuit of power in terms of how you will need to go about achieving your results. To be ruthless, you will need to have a heart of iron to accomplish this task. It will take a level of emotional training to learn how to master and control your emotions. A weak heart will often give in to emotions, which will only weaken and kill the ruthless spirit that you will need in your pursuit of power.

#3 - The Stoic Character

As you build your way up in power and even to maintain your position, you will need to play the stoic character. This is a role that will require you not to show your feelings or any form of emotional weakness. Unfortunately, in the dynamics of power, people will take advantage of your emotions and pull on your heartstrings if that is what will get them the results they need. I am not saying that you should keep your emotions built up inside of you, but there is a time and a place to unload your feelings. In the adversity of power is not the time or place to do so.

In the age of social media, where we have seen people make videos of themselves crying and showing too much vulnerability, they have gotten laughed at, mocked, and even ridiculed at times to the point where people have their vulnerability used against them as a tool of control. The purpose of the stoic character is to keep you in a state of rational thinking, logic, and sound reasoning in your decision making when building power.

#4 - The Revolutionary Character

Building power is a revolutionary act, which will require you to play the role of a revolutionary character. As we know, revolution is about change, which is what you will be doing in your pursuit of power. Sometimes change is necessary because a new generation is being born into the world that will have to adapt to the current social climate they are in, which may not be the same social climate that older generations were born and raised in.

Each new generation requires a revolution due to the constant evolution of social changes that occur over time. This means that what one generation may accept as the social norm, the new generation may reject. Hence why a call for revolutionary change may be needed, and this is where you use your revolutionary character to bring about revolutionary change when building power.

#5 - The Assertive Character

Being assertive is a character that you may need to tap into from time to time, especially if your position of power is a leadership role that will require you to assert yourself. In your position of power, you may need to use your assertiveness to communicate directly to people what it is you need. For example, as a leader in your position of power, it is important for you to voice any instructions that are needed to execute your mission. You will need to be confident in giving those instructions out to people without feeling any guilt or discomfort. You will take control and assert yourself as directly as possible to complete the task at hand.

#6 - The Risk-Taking Character

Taking risks is all a part of life. In the situation of building power, you will be required to take risks in order to achieve success. This is where you tap into your risk-taking character while you build power. Some of the moves and decisions you decide to make will be quite risky. There is no guarantee that things will always work out to your liking, but you will never know until you try. If it fails, you can gain a lesson from that failure and maybe approach that attempt again with a higher understanding of what you need to do better to gain the results you need.

Those that are in power today have had to take high-level risks to become who they are now, and their success would never have happened if they didn't take those risks. The philosophy here is: be prepared to take risks if you want to rise in your power. Do not let the fear of failure hold you back. Take the risk even if you are scared to do it. Push past the fear and proceed with your risk regardless.

#7 - The Confident Character

In your position of power, you will definitely need to carry a level of confidence. You will need to be confident in your approach to how you get things done. You will need to be confident in your decision making. Second-guessing yourself around your competitors will get you crushed in no time, as your competitors are very sure of themselves, so you will need to operate in the same manner if you are serious about rising in power.

Be confident in your abilities to execute your goals. Be confident to lead. Be confident in advising those that need your knowledge in the right direction, and always be willing to improve yourself, which will help to consistently raise your confidence levels up. Remember, without confidence, you will perish in the battlefield of power.

#8 - The Camouflage Character

The camouflage part of your character is what you will be required to use as a strategy to blend in with the masses so you go undetected until it is the correct time to strike when nobody sees you coming. You will pretend as if you are going along with social norms that are forced upon many of us, but you will secretly have your own agenda brewing in the background. You will slowly push out your agenda with logic, reasoning, and strategic movement with no premature, reactive, or explosive behaviour.

You will find that the camouflaged character is one of the most strategic methods you can use when you are building power. It is a strategy that allows you to go undetected in plain sight as you move around quietly without much disturbance.

#9 - The Selfish Character

The selfish character is a role you will also need to play at times. Unfortunately, you will not always be able to cater to others. Remember, you are not a machine. When you are in a position of power with a steady increase of influence, you may find that you will become in demand. This experience can get quite exhausting for you at times, and you may have to take some time out for yourself. This means you will have to put yourself first at some point, whether others like this or not. You are no use to others if you have no use to yourself. Make sure you always take care of yourself before you try to help others.

#10 - The Uncompromising Character

In the battlefield of power, you will need to be uncompromising in your stance of what it is you stand for, regardless of the odds, regardless of the discomfort that may bring to some people. You must not flinch or be moved by what others may say about your uncompromising character. What you will notice is that the small percentage of people in power operate in the same manner. You will also notice that society, to a degree, operates like this too, even though they may not admit it. It's not what people say; it's what their actions show.

In the battlefield of power, the uncompromising character comes with a level of force that commands respect. It shows that you are not willing to bend your stance under the pressures of adversity, whereas compromising only shows weakness in the eyes of the uncompromising characters of power. When you compromise, you only show that you are not in control. When you are seen as not being in control of the narrative or of any situation, you will be used and disposed of when you are no longer needed. You will only be used as a commodity.

So in order to succeed in the adversity of power, you will need to tap into the uncompromising side of your character, which is a tool you can use to keep yourself from being corrupted by others, especially your competitors.

Your Focus Is Not to Be Liked, but to Be Respected and Seen as Dangerous

On your pursuit of power, you must understand the reality of what this experience comes with, and one thing that must be understood is that it is not about being liked. It is about being respected and being seen as dangerous. Some may challenge this idea and ask how you can influence and be respected by anyone if they don't like you. The answer to that question is simple. First of all, it is not possible to be liked by everyone, so to even try and bend your character to please everybody is a waste of time and energy. People that tend to be liked in most cases are non-threatening and not seen as dangerous. Just because you are liked, it does not mean you are respected.

In the battlefield of power, it is not important to be liked. It is about who has the power and influence to enforce rules and narratives that people will follow. The aim here is not to focus on being liked, but to focus on being respected and being seen as dangerous. This means that people will have to think twice about attempting to cross your path, knowing they will have to pay the consequences.

Do Not Be Fooled by Constant Praises

On your journey to power, you may find that you may get praises from people. You see this on social media when some people display their success and you may see hundreds of comments of those people giving away praises, telling you congratulations. Now, on the surface level, this may seem admirable to you. You may even have a burst of energy when you see all those positive comments, but the truth is most of those comments are just empty words of hidden jealousy masked as positive celebration.

What we do not ask ourselves is: if the success is not coming from a collective standpoint and only benefits the individual, then how can one really embrace the success of that individual in the long term? People are forced with the narrative that they should embrace the success of others. What this does is create a knee-jerk reactive behaviour in most people to automatically congratulate those that are doing well, but in secret, they are not as happy for those people as they claim. Some of these people that praise you are holding a lot of jealous venom towards you, masked as a fake smile. Some of those people secretly want your position and may even backstab you to take your place.

The message here is: do not allow those praises to fool you. Do not fall for the hype of praises that surround you. If you allow the praises to make you believe that you are bigger than what you actually are, you risk the potential of creating a false sense of illusion in your mind about who you believe you are versus who you actually are in reality. Your aim is to stay grounded and focus on building power. Do not lose track because of mere praises you may receive from people. Remember, not every praise you receive is genuine. Also bear in mind that praises do not define who you are. Your character is the thing that defines you.

The Power in Rebuilding Yourself

In the dynamics of power, you will sometimes find that you may fall many times and will have to get yourself back up again. The thought of falling and having to rebuild from scratch may be scary for many, but having to rebuild again should be looked at as an opportunity for you to bounce back bigger, stronger, harder, and wiser. Also, rebuilding yourself can bring about character and a level of resilience about yourself you never knew existed, which can be used as an accelerating point of drive to propel yourself forward in your pursuit of power.

What most people do not know is that the more you fall and have to get back up and rebuild yourself, the easier it becomes. This is because you have fallen and bounced back many times, so you have a level of certainty as to what you are capable of doing if you are to ever fall flat on your face in the battlefield. The power in rebuilding yourself is that you can rebuild yourself in any way you want with no limitations. You are the creator of your new build of character. Remember, in the process of rebuilding yourself, do not allow the influence of others to dictate how you go about rebuilding your character. The rebuilding process must be in alignment with your purpose on your journey to building power in a manner that is recognisable to you and you only. It does not have to be understood by others.

Do Not Seek Revenge, Rise Above It and Continue the Mission

On your rise to power, make sure you use your strength wisely. Do not seek power to get revenge or to destroy others out of bitterness, rage, or anger. Unfortunately, there are some people that are still carrying the burden of grudges in their heart towards someone or people that may have done them wrong in the past. If you are the person that carries this burden in your heart and seek to carry out an act of revenge, I just want to warn you that it will be a waste of time and energy. In the end, you will only destroy yourself through your own emotional rage because instead of focusing on the mission of building power, you are focusing on a past event that has already taken place in your life, an event that you cannot change.

Instead, you can learn from that experience and use it as a tool of lessons that can make you wiser, sharper, and smarter. It is wise to rise above the idea of seeking revenge and continue your mission and other future endeavours. Do not allow the past hurts and pain to suffocate your present and your future. The philosophy of power does not encourage you to put wasted energy into petty acts of revenge, but to focus more on the building of power in your present and future existence on earth.

Do Not Rely on Motivational Speakers

On your journey to building power, it is important to be self-motivated. Be motivated by your own strengths. Be motivated by the struggles you have overcome in your life. Be motivated by your own success. Be motivated by your own will to rise regardless of the odds. Be motivated by your vision that you see very clearly. Allow all those things mentioned above to be your sense of motivation.

You do not need to waste time listening to motivational speakers that are not even living your current life experience. You do not need to waste time listening to countless motivational videos or speeches to revive your spirit. Ask yourself this: how can you be truly motivated by somebody who is not living your experience? How can you be motivated by somebody that does not share your struggles or challenges in life? The motivational speaker has a passion of their own that came from deep within themselves, and they chose to embark on their own personal journey to success. The excitement they carry is not your own, so you can never truly be motivated by them, even though you falsely tell yourself that they will be the one to get you off your feet.

Unfortunately, the motivational speaker does not tell you that you do not need them. They do motivational speeches, whether they go to schools, universities, or any other venue they go to perform their motivational speech. Some people will pay an expensive price to go and hear them deliver a speech, and the motivational speakers are happy to take your money in order for you to listen to them. You can't blame them for doing this, as that's how they make their money. It's a legitimate hustle, which I understand.

The thing I am trying to highlight here is that you are cheating yourself into believing that someone else is responsible for your own motivation. There is no power in trying to hijack someone else's motivation and making that your own. That is a crime towards yourself. The philosophy of building power does not encourage you to engage in a false sense of motivation from someone else's motivational speech. The philosophy of building power encourages you to be your own motivational speaker to yourself, to speak life into your goals, speak life into your vision, and finally be motivated by your own will and determination to succeed at what you set out to do on your journey to building power.

ABOUT THE AUTHOR

Courtney Sharpe was born and raised in Birmingham, UK, on October 14th, 1983, to Jamaican parents. Growing up as the middle child in a family of six siblings — three brothers and three sisters — Courtney learned early on the value of staying grounded and level-headed. His keen sense of observation of the world around him shaped his understanding of society, which has become a central theme in his writing.

Courtney is also the author of How to Survive in Babylon, a sensational self-help book that speaks directly to the challenges faced by those navigating life in a system designed to limit their potential.

His journey from childhood to adulthood has been filled with rich experiences that have contributed to his depth of character and consciousness. By the age of 25, he embarked on a revolutionary journey, developing a heightened sense of awareness about the struggles faced by individuals in modern society, which he often refers to as "Babylon." His revolutionary thought process, inspired by teachings and personal experiences, flows through the pages of his writing, offering insights and guidance for those navigating life's complexities.

Driven by a deep mission to uplift those who find it difficult to navigate through Babylon's challenges, Courtney's work speaks to the everyday struggler, offering wisdom, clarity, and empowerment. His writing is not just about survival but about overcoming and thriving, with a revolutionary spirit that challenges the status quo.

Courtney Sharpe continues to write with purpose and passion, aiming to inspire and bring about change, one reader at a time.

Visit Courtney's website

www.ingramcontent.com/pod-product-compliance
Lightning Source LLC
Chambersburg PA
CBHW071149120626
46546CB00006B/2190